BERKSHIRE OUTDOORS

Bike Rides

Bike Rides

IN THE BERKSHIRE HILLS
Revised and Updated Edition

TEXT BY LEWIS C. CUYLER

Bicycle Route Maps by Nellie Fink
Berkshire County Map by Vaughan Gray
and Ron Toelke Associates

BERKSHIRE HOUSE PUBLISHERS
Stockbridge, Massachusetts

Text designed and composed by Jane McWhorter, using Palatino and Helvetica typefaces. Cover photograph © Dan McCoy/ Rainbow. Bicycle route maps by Nellie Fink. Berkshire County map by Ron Toelke Associates, based on an original by Vaughan Gray.

Library of Congress Cataloging-in-Publication Data
Cuyler, Lewis C.
Bike rides in the Berkshire Hills / text by Lewis C. Cuyler ; bicycle route maps by Nellie Fink ; Berkshire County map by Vaughan Gray and Ron Toelke Associates. — Rev. and updated ed.
p.   cm.
Includes bibliographical references.
ISBN 0-936399-68-6 : $9.95
1. Bicycle touring—Massachusetts—Berkshire Hills—Guidebooks.
2. Berkshire Hills (Mass.)—Guidebooks. I. Title. II. Series.
GV1045.5.M42B4725   1995
796.6′4′097441—dc20   94-41377
                                                                        CIP

ISBN: 0-936399-68-6

Editors: David Emblidge and Virginia Rowe

Berkshire House Publishers
Box 297
Stockbridge, Massachusetts 01262

Manufactured in the United States of America

First printing 1995
10 9 8 7 6 5 4 3 2 1

BERKSHIRE OUTDOORS

. . . is a series of recreation books for the Berkshire County region of Western Massachusetts. Berkshire Outdoor titles are designed for both novices and experts — occasional enthusiasts and every-day exercisers in several sports, as well as devotees of Berkshire County's natural settings, flora, and fauna. Current titles include the book you hold in your hand as well as *Hikes & Walks in the Berkshire Hills* (by Lauren R. Stevens), *Skiing (Downhill & Cross Country) in the Berkshire Hills* (by Lauren R. Stevens and Lewis C. Cuyler), *Natural Places in the Berkshires* (by René Laubach), and *Wildflowers of the Berkshire and Taconic Hills* (by Joseph G. Strauch, Jr.). The series is dedicated to inspiring respect for the beauty and continued good health of Berkshire's natural environment.

To Harriet

BERKSHIRE, THE BERKSHIRES, THE BERKSHIRE HILLS

What is the name of this place, anyway ? The original Berkshire is in England, south of Oxford. There it's pronounced "Bark-sheer." Presumably it was a tanning center, for "berk" derives from "bark," used to make leather. "Shire" means "hilly country county." Certainly trees and hills distinguish Berkshire County in America.

Purists refer to the "Berkshire Hills," meaning specifically what this book calls the southern Taconics, including peaks in New York State. The logic of calling all hills in Berkshire County the Berkshire Hills seems to be gaining acceptance.

"The Berkshires" is a 20th-century term used to publicize the county. This book avoids it, favoring instead just "Berkshire County" or, even more simply, "Berkshire."

TABLE OF CONTENTS

BIKE RIDES

SOUTH COUNTY

From Gt. Barrington South:

Estates and Industry:

CENTRAL COUNTY

Lenox: More Estates:

Pittsfield: Berkshire's Urban Place 112

NORTH COUNTY

Mt. Greylock: Head for the Sky 141

Northern Berkshire: Mountains, Mills, Art and
Education 149

LIST OF MAPS

Regional map, 16
County divisions, 19
Berkshire Access maps, 21-22
Relief map, 36

INTRODUCTION

In the three years since the publication of this book's first edition, Berkshire roads and scenery haven't changed much, but bicycling has become much more popular as an activity for fun and exercise.

The scale of the Berkshires is an exact fit for bicyclists, whose sensuous pace is ideal for full discovery of the county's understated elegance and its historical and present-day cultural richness. Civilization is never far away from the county's miles of secondary roads that snake their way through gentle finger-shaped valleys and misty hills. Just by riding, bicyclists savor sights, sounds and smells in a way unknown to travelers restricted by the confines of a car.

In the Berkshires, as elsewhere, bicycling requires neither excessive strength, agility nor speed. Almost anyone can ride; it just takes doing. In the initial stages of learning, as once pointed out by bicycle-touring guru John S. Freiden, riders are like caterpillars. Every hill is large and every speed is slow. But riders soon become butterflies, floating effortlessly over hills, and in the process of transformation they find their senses awakened. Riding puts them in touch with feelings, both mental and physical, routinely suppressed during their daily lives.

Of course, bicycling isn't always perfect in Berkshire County. As in other places bicycling here has its good and bad moments. They range from the sublime, such as the easy ride south through the vibrant green corridor of Monument Valley Road on a morning in early June, to the raw and uncomfortable, as when a sudden storm angrily develops on Mt. Greylock, halfway up a bicycle climb in mid-August.

Mostly, however, the extremes are gently blended into an adventure with the ever-present anticipation of discovering what's over the next hill or around the next curve. In the process bicycle tourers discover that by slowing down, they gain control over the speed of life. As a result, they take as much pleasure in the going as in the arriving.

Berkshire County has about 132,000 people who live in

two modestly sized cities and 30 towns spread out over 947 square miles in a rectangular shape at the western end of Massachusetts. Bounded roughly by the Hoosac mountain range on the east, the Taconic range on the west, dominated in the north by Mt. Greylock — at 3,491 feet the state's highest peak — and in the south by Mt. Everett, the county has always stood slightly apart from its neighbors. This is more a matter of geography than the official boundaries that separate the Berkshires from the rest of Massachusetts and the neighboring states of Vermont, New York and Connecticut. Geography has shaped Berkshire history; and bicyclists, as riders of machines that must constantly interact with the terrain, are particularly equipped to see how this is true.

Because the county is hilly, Berkshire bicycling is definitely not for those who like all of their riding flat. In fact, none of the rides in the guide can be described as level. Rather, most are rolling, consisting of gradual uphills or downhills, with a few steep mountains in between. The mountains, however, are never large enough to prevent good bicycling, and roads follow the valleys in such a way that any bicyclist in good shape and using a bike geared for 10 speeds or more will be rewarded by tours that are among the most scenic in New England. Many of the rides described offer more points of interest per square mile than just about anywhere else in the country.

This book will guide you — on two wheels — all around the roads of Berkshire County, following essentially the same pattern as its predecessor. I hope you enjoy reading about the trips as much as I have enjoyed writing about them. Better yet, I hope you can ride some of them, and thus discover a Berkshire County you will never really see by car. In doing so, may I wish for the wind always to be at your back and for your hills always to be down, as the old greeting goes. I know too well that neither hills nor wind will always behave that way in Berkshire County, but nevertheless I am confident its other offerings will compensate.

HOW TO USE THIS BOOK

This book tries to be accurate and helpful. Neither the author nor the publisher can be responsible beyond that effort. Many things, both natural and manmade, are subject to change and out of the author's control. And, with the best intentions, errors are possible.

As prospective bicycle tourists will see, none of the individual rides described here takes more than a day. Attempts have been made to make all of the trips loops, to route them all on secondary roads with hard surfaces and still cover the county's major points of interest. They do not cover every town, and many places not mentioned make rewarding visits.

Care has been taken to make the distances mentioned accurate, but no two odometers ever seem to read the same, so the readings must be taken as close approximations. To obtain the most benefit from this guide, you should equip your bicycle with an odometer.

As with any guidebook, the rides described represent only starting points. A careful study of a county map will show how they relate and how they can be varied or combined to accommodate a trip's needs.

Additional Maps

To find some of the not-so-obvious corners of the county, a supplement to regular road maps is advisable. One is Jimapco Map C12, Berkshire County, MA, 4th edition, $3.25. It is available in bookstores, drugstores, and newspaper stores or from Jimapco, Box 1137, Clifton Park, NY 12065; 1-800-MAPS 123. The most detailed map of county roads is available for $5 from the Berkshire County Commission, County Courthouse, 76 East St., Pittsfield, MA 01201. The courthouse is on Park Square, where the Pittsfield rides originate. For an extra charge, the commission will mail the maps to you. The maps are also available from the Southern Berkshire Registry of Deeds, 334 Main St., Gt. Barrington. There is also a 1990 city street and Berkshire County Historical Map available for $1.50

from the Central Berkshire Chamber of Commerce, 66 West St., Pittsfield.

Conventional road maps are also helpful but sometimes omit details needed by bicyclists. Another good bet is the Massachusetts tourist map published by the Massachusetts Office of Travel & Tourism, 100 Cambridge St., Boston, MA 02202. Call 1-800-447-MASS, ext. 500. In Pittsfield, county maps are available from the Berkshire Visitors Bureau, 50 South St., in the Berkshire Hilton complex.

Organization

Following a generally accepted tradition, this book is organized in three parts: South, Central, and North County, as shown on the adjacent map. That should be a help in locating the rides closest to you. Here is a plug, however; try some farther removed. Differences exist, interesting in their own right and helpful in defining the characteristics of the rides with which you are most familiar.

Ride descriptions include the rural areas surrounding Sheffield, Gt. Barrington and West Stockbridge; the estate towns of Lenox and Stockbridge; the city of Pittsfield; and Mt. Greylock and points north, where the mountains are steeper and the valleys narrower. A final section suggests linking routes among all the trips, and the appendices offer advice on various practical matters around biking.

NORTH COUNTY
Adams (Population: 9,340)
Cheshire (3,489)
Clarksburg (1,779)
Florida (735)
New Ashford (226)
North Adams (14,535)
Savoy (683)
Williamstown (8,378)

CENTRAL COUNTY
Becket (1,876)
Dalton (7,074)
Hancock (651)
Hinsdale (2,025)
Lanesborough (3,005)
Lenox (5,600)
Peru (832)
Pittsfield (42,229)
Richmond (1,696)
Washington (615)
Windsor (845)

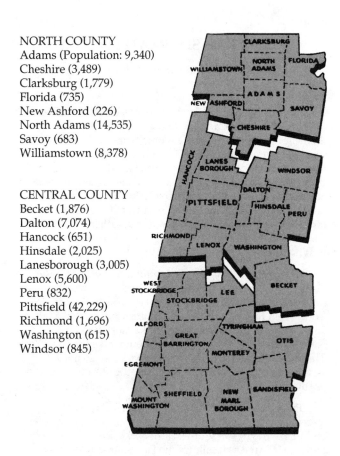

SOUTH COUNTY
Alford (418)
Egremont (1,152)
Great Barrington (7,416)
Lee (5,898)
Monterey (918)
Mount Washington (135)
New Marlborough (918)
Otis (1,200)
Sandisfield (809)
Sheffield (2,967)
Stockbridge (2,450)
Tyringham (348)
West Stockbridge (1,475)

TRANSPORTATION

Getting to the Berkshires

BY CAR

From Manhattan: Take the Major Deegan Expressway or the Henry Hudson Parkway to the Saw Mill River Parkway, then proceed north on the Taconic State Parkway. For the southern Berkshires, exit the Taconic at Hillsdale, Claverack, Rte. 23 and follow 23 east, towards Hillsdale and on to Gt. Barrington. For Stockbridge, Lee, and Lenox, (and all points in South and Central county) proceed up Rte. 7. For Williamstown and all of northern Berkshire, you might want to proceed farther up the Taconic and exit at Rte. 295, then Rte. 22 north, leading to Stephentown, then follow Rte. 43 through Hancock to Williamstown.

From New Jersey, Pennsylvania and the South: Rte. 22 north is a good choice for local color, and you can pick it up as far south as Armonk or Bedford in Westchester County, New York. From Rte. 22, farther upstate, turn right at Hillsdale on 23 east toward Gt. Barrington. For the most direct route from New Jersey, Pennsylvania and the South, take the New York Thruway to I-84 east; at the Taconic parkway go north to Rte. 23 for southern Berkshire or Rte. 295, Rte. 22 and Rte. 43 for northern Berkshire.

From Connecticut and/or New York Metro Area: Rte. 7 is a scenic route, which can be picked up at Danbury, via I-684 and I-84. To arrive in southeastern Berkshire, Rte. 8 is a quick and scenic drive as it follows the Farmington River north.

From Boston and the East: The Massachusetts Turnpike is the quickest, easiest and one of the more scenic routes west to southern Berkshire. West of the Connecticut River, you can get off the turnpike at Exit 3 and take Rte. 202 south to Rte. 20 west and pick up Rte. 23 west at Woronoco for the best route to Otis Ridge, Butternut Basin and Catamount ski areas. Most people stay on the turnpike right into Berkshire County, exiting either at Lee or West Stockbridge. *(Continued on pg. 23)*

BERKSHIRE ACCESS

Using Tanglewood (on the Stockbridge — Lenox line) as the Berkshire reference point, the following cities are this close.

CITY	TIME	MILES
Albany	1 hr	50
Boston	2 1/2 hrs	135
Bridgeport	2 hrs	110
Danbury	1 3/4 hrs	85
Hartford	1 1/2 hrs	70
Montreal	5 hrs	275
New Haven	2 1/2 hrs	115
New York City	3 hrs	150
Philadelphia	4 1/2 hrs	230
Providence	2 1/2 hrs	125
Springfield	3/4 hr	35
Waterbury	1 1/2 hrs	75
Washington, DC	7 hrs	350
Worcester	1 3/4 hrs	90

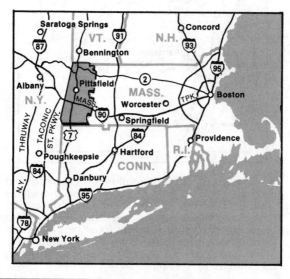

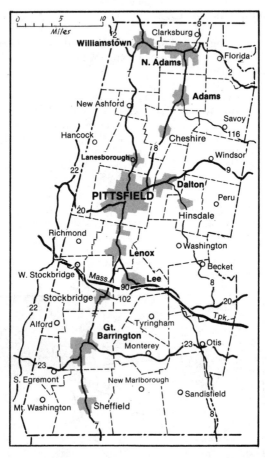

Berkshire County is 56 miles south to north, from Sheffield to Williamstown. Depending on the season and the weather, it's normally a two-hour leisurely drive up Rte. 7. Because of the mountain ranges that run along this route, east-west travel across the county remains much more difficult, with all the county's east-west routes (2 in the north; 9, midcounty; and 23 in the south) being tricky drives in freezing or snowy weather.

(Continued from pg. 20)

If you're coming west to the Berkshires from more northern latitudes, eastern entry to Berkshire County can be gained by driving the original Mohawk Trail, an Indian byway. Also known as Rte. 2, this is the most direct way to Jiminy Peak and Brodie Mountain skiing .

From Hartford: The quickest route by far is I-91 north to the Massachusetts Turnpike west. Then proceed as in directions for Massachusetts Turnpike travel from Boston.

From Montreal or Albany: Leaving Canada, take I-87 (known as "the Northway") south to Albany, and exit at Rte. 7 to Rte. 2 toward Williamstown, or continue on I-87 south to I-90 east, connecting then to the Massachusetts Turnpike which is the continuation of I-90 east. Exit at either Canaan, New York, or Lee, Massachusetts.

BY BUS
Please note: Schedules and prices are subject to change. We advise that you call ahead to check.

From Manhattan (3.5 hours): Bonanza (212-947-1766; 800-556-3815) serves the Berkshires out of New York City's Port Authority Bus Terminal (212-564-8484) between 40th and 41st St. and 8th and 9th Aves. Tickets may be purchased at the Adirondack Trailways ticket windows, near 8th Ave. Boarding is down the escalators at the center of the terminal, and then to the right, usually at Gate 13. Bonanza runs three buses daily: 8:45 a.m., 2:15 p.m., and 5:15 p.m. There is also an additional Friday evening bus, leaving Port Authority at 7:30. The 1994 round-trip ticket price was $52 to Great Barrington; one way was $26. Berkshire locales marked with an asterisk are Flag Stops, where you must wave to the bus driver in order to be picked up.

Berkshire Phone Numbers for New York Buses

Canaan, CT	Canaan Pharmacy, Main St.	 203-824-5481
Gt. Barrington	Bill's Pharmacy, 362 Main St.	 413-528-1590
Hillsdale, NY	*Junction Rtes. 22 & 23	 800-556-3815

Lee	McClelland Drugs, 43 Main St. 413-243-0135
Lenox	Lenox News & Variety,
	39 Housatonic St. 413-637-2815
New Ashford	*Entrance to Brodie Mt. Ski Area,
	Rte. 7 800-556-3815
Pittsfield	Bus Terminal, 57 S. Church St. 413-442-4451
Sheffield	*First Agricultural Bank, Rte. 7 800-556-3815
S. Egremont	*Gaslight Store 800-556-3815
Stockbridge	Stockbridge Information Booth,
	Main St. 800-556-3815
Williamstown	Williams Inn, Main St. 413-458-2665

From Boston (3.5 hours): Peter Pan serves the Berkshires from Boston out of the Peter Pan/Trailways Bus Terminal, 555 Atlantic Ave. (800-237-8747, 800-343-9999, 617-426-7838). There are six arrivals and departures daily from Pittsfield. In 1994 a round trip was $47.80; one way was $23.90. Berkshire-bound passengers change buses at Springfield. There are two buses daily to Williamstown and North Adams. The Pittsfield terminal is at 57 South Church St. (413-442-4451).

Berkshire Phone Numbers for Boston Buses

Lee	McClelland Drugs, 43 Main St. 413-243-0135
Lenox	Lenox News & Variety,
	39 Housatonic St. 413-637-2815
Pittsfield	Bus Terminal, 57 S. Church St. 413-442-4451
Williamstown	Williams Inn, 1090 Main St. 413-458-2665
N.Adams	Oasis Plaza,
	148 American Legion Dr. 800-343-9999

From Hartford (1.75 hours): Peter Pan runs 2 buses and Bonanza runs 4 buses to Pittsfield daily from Union Station at 1 Union Place, Hartford (203-724-5400). The 1994 round-trip ticket price was $31.95.

From Montreal (6 hours): Greyhound runs south to the Albany Greyhound Terminal. Connect to Pittsfield as noted below.

From Albany (1 hour):   Peter Pan runs 3 buses and Bonanza runs two buses daily from Albany to Pittsfield; 1994 round-trip ticket was $15 on both lines.

BY TRAIN

From Manhattan: Amtrak (800-USA-RAIL or 413-872-7245) can help you get to the Berkshires, but not all the way. Ticket prices vary, so call Amtrak for up-to-date information. The Amtrak turboliner from Penn Station runs frequently and smoothly along the Hudson River. For southern Berkshire, stay aboard till Hudson; for northern Berkshire, carry on to Rensselaer. Limousine or taxi service can be arranged for the 40-mi. trip from Hudson to southern Berkshire or from Rensselaer to northern Berkshire (46 mi.); see information below under "By Taxi or Limousine."

From Boston: Amtrak runs a single train daily through the Berkshires, starting from Boston's South Station. The Pittsfield depot has no actual station; it's just a shelter. (To find the depot: take West St. westwards past the Hilton; at the first light, turn right onto Center St.; take the next right onto Depot St.; the shelter is on the left.)   Anyone boarding the train in Pittsfield must purchase tickets on the train or from a travel agency. The 1994 round-trip ticket prices ranged from $27 each way to $42–$54 round trip, depending on time of travel and seat availability. Private compartments are available, ranging from $48 supplementary for a single compartment to $82 supplementary for a double compartment.

From Montreal: Amtrak runs one train daily from Montreal through Albany. The 1994 round-trip ticket price was $50–$98, excluding holiday periods. During the Thanksgiving, Christmas, and New Year's seasons, the round-trip rate rises to $98. There is a same-day train connection from this run to the Berkshires; see below.

From Albany: Amtrak has a single Pittsfield-bound train daily from the Albany/Rensselaer Depot on East St. (2 miles from downtown Albany). The 1994 ticket fare was $10 one

way, and ranges from $16 to $20 round trip depending on time
of travel and seat availability.

BY PLANE

If you own a small airplane or decide to charter one, you
can fly directly to the Berkshires, landing at Gt. Barrington,
Pittsfield or N. Adams airports.

From New York City: There are several charter air
companies in the metropolitan New York area that will fly you
from La Guardia, JFK or other airports near New York to any
of the Berkshire airports. Their 1994 estimated rates ran from
$400 to $2100 one way, for a twin-engine airplane (holds five
plus the pilot). A jet with two pilots was considerably more.
Airlines currently flying these routes include:

      Aircraft Charter Group 800-553-3590
      Chester Air, Chester, CT 800-752-6371
      Long Island Airways 800-645-9572

and from Westchester County:

      Panorama (White Plains airport) 914-328-9800
         if calling from New York City: 718-507-9800
      Richmor Aviation 800-331-6101

From Boston: Estimated rates for 1994 ran $400 to $690 for
a twin-engine airplane (holds five plus the pilot).

      Bird Airfleet 508-372-6566
      Wiggins Airways . . . . 617-762-5690 Ext. #251

From Hartford: Bradley Airport in Hartford handles
numerous domestic and international airlines, so you can fly
to Bradley from nearly anywhere. From there, charter air
service to the Berkshires is available through any of the
companies listed under "From Boston" or through the Berkshire
County companies listed below.

From Albany: Albany is terminus for a substantial volume of domestic jet traffic and, being under an hour from the Berkshires by car, is the closest you can get to these hills by jet. Charter connector flights from Albany to the Berkshires are available through Page Flight (800-CHARTER) or through the Berkshire County companies listed below.

In Berkshire County: There are three aviation companies in Berkshire County which operate air taxi service to just about any other northeastern airport.

> Berkshire Aviation . . . . . . .Gt. Barrington Airport
> 413-528-1010 or -528-1061
> Lyon Aviation . . . . .Pittsfield Airport
> 413-443-6700
> Esposito Flying Service . . . .Harriman & West Airport
> N. Adams
> 413-663-3330

These local carriers' 1994 rates for a twin-engine plane (holds five plus the pilot) averaged $165 to Albany, $515 to Boston, $215 to Hartford, $620 to La Guardia or JFK, and $585 to Teterboro, New Jersey (at the foot of the George Washington Bridge). They also have single-engine planes (holds three plus pilot) for roughly 35-40% less, but these are dependent on weather conditions.

BY LIMOUSINE OR TAXI

There are many limousine services which will whisk you away from urban gridlock to the spaciousness of this hill country. From Hartford's Bradley Airport and Albany Airport, fares tend to be figured by the hour, with a three-hour minimum, and in 1994 ran anywhere from $120 to $250 from Hartford and $110 to $155 from Albany. Boston and New York fares are figured by the mile and 1994 rates vary from $1.25 to $1.60 per mile, plus gratuities, tolls, and parking. Total cost would include the return mileage for the limousine. (See mileage chart at the beginning of "Berkshire Access.")

From New York and its Airports:
>   Kabot . . . . .718-545-2400 or 413-626-3700
>   Esquire . . . . .212-935-9700 or 413-737-7000

From Boston and Logan Airport:
>   Cooper . . . . .617-482-1000 or 800-342-2123
>   Fifth Avenue 617-286-0555

From Hartford and Bradley Airport:
>   Carey, Aster Madison Avenue . .800-RE:LIMOS
>   Ambassador 203-633-7300
>   or 800-395-LIMO
>   Buckley .203-953-8787
>   Elite 203-223-4423

From Albany, Albany Airport and Rensselaer:
>   AAA Limousine Service 518-456-5030
>   Diamond Limousine 518-283-8000

>   To northern Berkshire (by reservation only):
>   Norm's Limousine Service 413-663-8300
>   or 413-663-6284

From Hudson, NY and its Amtrak Station:
>   Star City Taxi 518-828-3355

LODGING AND DINING

Berkshire offers a host of possibilities for lodging and dining, from the humble to the luxurious. The popularity of the area as a tourist destination means that those who want to visit in busy seasons must plan ahead. Lodging reservations are particularly important. We recommend two approaches to finding a place to stay and deciding where to eat. *The Berkshire Book: A Complete Guide*, by Jonathan Sternfield, from the publishers of this biking guide, is a thoroughly researched travel book, covering not only lodging and dining, but culture, recreation, shopping and many other topics as well. *The New York Times* said its recommendations were "right on the money." It is available from bookstores throughout the United States or from the publisher (Berkshire House, Box 297, Stockbridge, MA 01262; $16.95). Or you can call the Berkshire Visitors Bureau (413-443-9186) to ask for their package of brochures about lodging and dining possibilities. Both *The Berkshire Book* and the Visitors Bureau provide telephone numbers for Chamber of Commerce and other lodging reservations services.

Jonathan Sternfield's *The Berkshire Book* actually reviews restaurants and food purveyors, and you might enjoy seeing whether your opinions harmonize with his.

Camping in State Parks and Forests

Camping is offered at both private campgrounds and in 10 of the county's 14 state parks. Six state parks, within close bicycling range of the routes described in this book, are Beartown (Monterey), Clarksburg (Clarksburg), Mt. Greylock (Adams and Lanesborough), Pittsfield State Forest, October Mtn. (Lee) and Sandisfield State Forest.

Specific information about all of the state parks and forests in the county may be obtained from Dept. of Environmental Management, Div. of Forests and Parks, Region Five HQ, Box 1433, Pittsfield, MA 01201; 413-442-8928.

SAFETY

No matter the style of bicycling, off-road or on-road, riders must concern themselves with safety and the possibility of emergencies.

Riders should never forget that bicycles are no match for cars, trucks and buses. Therefore, it is imperative to ride on the right side of the road, single file, use a rearview mirror of some sort to see what is coming up from behind, and, most important of all, wear a helmet.

Modern bicycle helmets are lightweight, well ventilated and provide protection from both sun and rain. While they represent an extra cost, the investment is so minimal as to be nonexistent when compared to the medical costs for head injuries, not to mention emotional trauma.

Always check the brakes before starting a trip. If it's raining, ride defensively because brakes simply don't hold as well when they are wet. One of the real panic-prompters in bicycling is to squeeze the brakes in a rain emergency and have nothing happen. It's a good idea to test brakes frequently when it's raining and if the rain is light enough such tests will dry the rims somewhat.

Most other safety practices are grounded in common sense. Obey stop signs and traffic lights. Again, a bicycle is no match for a car or truck.

Wear bright colors. After dark, the state requires a headlight, a red rear reflector, as well as side and pedal reflectors.

Use hand signals when turning in traffic. Left turns are easy. To signal a right turn, extend your right arm and point. Motorists will get the "point."

Avoid storm sewers with grates. Their openings may match the direction of the bicycle wheel. If they do, they will trap the wheel, sending the rider head over handlebars.

Remember that bridges with riding decks of iron grillwork are extremely slippery when wet. Even when dry, they make steering difficult.

Watch out for railroad tracks. Take them at a right angle, never diagonally.

Be careful of wet leaves in the fall. They are slippery.

And don't panic if chased by a dog, one of the most common of all bicycle problems. You can usually outride the dog, since dogs are territorial in nature. Often modern dogs aren't in very good shape anyway and simply can't keep up. Remember that if you keep your legs spinning it will make it very difficult for the dog to bite. Many dogs are discouraged by sharp words telling them to back off. A rap on the snout with a bicycle pump can also stop a dog in its tracks, so can a squirt from a water bottle. And if you have to dismount, keep your bicycle between you and the dog, using it as a fence. Smile and try to keep a sense of humor.

And finally, take along a first-aid kit with a few Band Aids, some gauze, antiseptic ointment and a couple of absorbent pads. Add sunburn lotion and bug repellent.

WEATHER

Climate

"If you don't like the weather in New England, wait five minutes. . . ." That was Mark Twain's opinion (he summered in Tyringham), and there are plenty of days when his exaggeration seems pretty close to reality. How the Berkshire climate strikes you depends on what you're used to. People visiting from outside the region may be helped by the following information.

In general, while summers are blessedly mild due to the elevation of the Berkshire hills, summer visitors should remember that nights can be quite cool; bring sweaters.

Average Temperature
October	48.4°
January	20.4°
April	43.4°
July	68.3°

Average Annual Precipitation
Rainfall plus water content of snow 44.15"
Snow   75.7"

Weather Reports
| Great Barrington | 413-528-1118 |
| Pittsfield | 413-499-2627 |

BERKSHIRE HISTORY

Both natural history and social history in Berkshire are tales of ups and downs. Looking at both from the end of the 20th century, you may feel some past time was better than the present, but it ain't necessarily so. The county testifies that geography, for all our veneer of civilization, is still destiny. And this county, now, maintains a delicate balance of being close to but not too close to the Boston–Washington megalopolis that holds down the East Coast. It is an accessible hinterland. It has the position and the resources to rise up into the future.

Six hundred million years ago the area was down, under the ocean, which was at work forming the rocks. It was warm and wet, with sandy beaches and clear, shallow waters. The lapping waves built up beaches that turned to sandstone, which in turn metamorphosed into quartzite — the erosion-resistant backbone of many of the county's ridges. Shelled marine animals built coral reefs, which calcified into limestone. The deposits of this alkaline agent, mined on the side of Mt. Greylock in Adams, protect the area from the worst ravages of acid precipitation today. Some of that limestone was recrystalized into marble, snowy chunks of which grace the hiking trails and can be inspected at the Natural Bridge in Clarksburg. Muddy offshore sediments settled to form shales and then schists, crystalline rocks that fracture cleanly. The bands of granite that run through the southern part of the county antedate the metamorphic rock.

The continents began to shift, in response to subterranean pressure. At a speed of about an inch a year over 150 million years, the land masses that would one day be North America, Africa, and Europe moved towards each other, closing the proto-Atlantic ocean. Several arcs of offshore volcanic islands were shoved onto the continent by a series of slow but cataclysmic collisions known as the Taconic Orogeny (Taconic mountain building). The entire continental shelf was squeezed into a series of folds, the monumental forerunners of the Appalachian Range. The bases of these mountains, some Himalayan in height, must have just about filled Berkshire, when the county reached for the sky. Then the continents began to pull apart, as they are still doing.

As soon as mountains were stacked up, the process of erosion began. Rain fell, forming rivers that still drain these hills, but in those days more vigorously carving a land-scape unrooted by vegetation. Not only water but wind sculpted Berkshire hills, raging unbroken by trees and shrubs. The rugged landscape was tamed, waiting only for plants to soften it.

Less than two million years ago the first of a succession of four ice sheets ground down in response to a cooling climate. These mile-high glaciers brought debris, gravel and rocks, which they deposited around the nubbins of mountains that remained. Glacial lakes covered most of North County and a good portion of the south. Because the Hoosac Valley was preglacial, once the melt set in, the Hoosic River returned to flowing across the north-south path of the ice. This and the Upper Ammonoosuc in New Hampshire are the only rivers in New England to flow from southwest to northeast. Nor were the beds of the Housatonic or Westfield much altered. The Farmington River ran up against a load of glacial trash that turned its general southerly course in Connecticut.

The ice withdrew as recently as 10,000 years ago. Vegetation and then wildlife followed its retreating edge. Perhaps a few of the earliest North American inhabitants, having boated or walked across the land bridge from Asia, were in Berkshire to bid farewell to the ice. Gradually, the evergreen forest moved north, lingering only on the tops of   the highest ridges, while the broad-leaved, deciduous forest moved in, characterized in North County by sugar maple and in the south by oak, with their associated pines, ash, beech, birch and alder.

The rocky steepness of the county does not lend itself to leisurely flowing water and big lakes. With the exception of the southern reach of the Housatonic, which meanders in curlicues through Sheffield, Berkshire rivers retain little water and rush to their destinations. What lakes the county has, it owes to the efforts of 19th-century industrialists to create a head or a reservoir to provide a year-round flow of water for power or other manufacturing processes: Otis Reservoir, Cheshire Reservoir, Pontoosuc, Onota, and others.

Seen from above, the county presents the ridges that remain from the north-south running folds, the Taconics along the New York line, the lower end of the Green Mountains protruding over the Vermont line, the Hoosacs filling the northeast quadrant, the Southern Berkshire Plateau filling the southeast quadrant, and a line of river valleys, just to the left of center, made up of the Hoosic and Housatonic — albeit flowing in opposite directions — that meet in New Ashford.

The Greylock massif stands as a peninsula to the Taconics — as indeed it was when glacial Lake Bascom filled the Hoosac Valley up to the 1,300-ft. contour. Therefore it may be appropriate that the summit of Greylock lifts a War Memorial Tower, designed originally to be a lighthouse for the Charles River estuary, bearing a beacon that can be seen by people navigating most of the county. If any man-made feature is needed to unite a geographical area so well defined topographically, it would be that tower and the roads it guards (Rtes. 2, 7 and 8).

Getting in and out and around Berkshire used to be a problem. The native Americans generally thought of the area as removed from their Hudson River homes, a hunting ground to visit in the summer. The Mahicans entered from the south or north, along the river valleys. Although the Bay Colony claimed the land early on, Bay Colony residents found it tough to surmount the Berkshire barrier to the east. Early settlers found it easier to enter along the valleys, a few Dutch infiltrating through the Taconics from New York, but especially residents from the area now known as Connecticut, up the Housatonic. Thus the county was settled from the south to the north, the earliest towns in the south dating to the first quarter of the 18th century. The main roads, railroads and even sewer lines now follow the valleys.

The European settlers were primarily farmers, typically working the bottom lands and, as they filled up, moving up the sides of the hills. Remains of walls, cellar holes, and orchards such as you come across in your ambles remind you that even what seem now lofty ridges were at one time home,

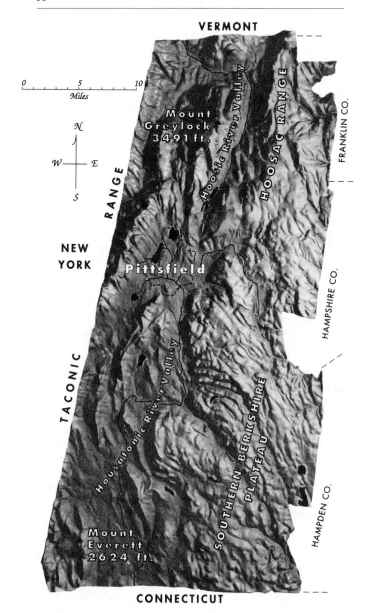

VERMONT

0   5   10
Miles

N

W — *E*

S

Mount
Greylock
3491 ft.

Hoosic River Valley

HOOSAC RANGE

FRANKLIN CO.

**NEW
YORK**

Pittsfield

RANGE

HAMPSHIRE CO.

TACONIC

Housatonic River Valley

SOUTHERN BERKSHIRE
PLATEAU

HAMPDEN CO.

Mount
Everett
2624 ft.

CONNECTICUT

especially for those who made their living grazing cattle or merino sheep. In Stockbridge, the English Society for the Propagation of the Gospel in Foreign Parts set up an Indian mission, which gradually acceded to the land hunger of the Europeans. By the time of the Revolution, virtually all native Americans had departed.

As a farmer installed a mill to grind his corn or saw his wood, and his neighbors came to have him do their milling, so industry followed the plough. What began as groupings to protect against French or Indian raids became trading centers. Specialty manufactures, depending on natural resources, developed, such as glass, paper, charcoal, and textiles. Even education can be seen as an industry depending on natural resources. After all, Thoreau said of Williams College's position at the foot of Greylock: "It would be no small advantage if every college were thus located at the base of a mountain, as good at least as one well-endowed professorship . . . . Some will remember, no doubt, not only that they went to college, but that they went to the mountain." In Berkshire County, three of the four colleges and many of the secondary schools are at the base of mountains.

The opening of the Erie Canal in 1825, providing a practical means for younger residents to head west where the thick topsoil had a lot fewer glacial stones than that of Berkshire, drained the county of human resources. One by one lights winked out on the sidehill farms. Whereas by the middle of the century three-quarters of the trees had been stripped for pasture land or to feed the insatiable maws of the railroad, the county has been revegetating for 150 years. In Berkshire that ratio is inverted today. The county is three-quarters wooded, which is why coyotes, bear, beaver, turkeys, and even moose are returning to join the populous deer and smaller animals.

The most important industrial event in the county's history happened in 1886, when William Stanley linked 25 shops along the main street of Great Barrington in the world's first commercial electric system. That, in turn, drew the General Electric Co. to Stanley's shop in Pittsfield. GE has been here ever since, the largest employer in the county. The second most important industrial event was the opening of the Hoosac

Tunnel, at 4.75 miles the longest bore in the world in 1875, breaking through the Berkshire barrier for direct train service in the North County from Boston to Albany.

Yet even in the heady days when industry was king — the population of Pittsfield growing from 25,000 to 58,000 in the first 60 years of the 20th century — second homes, tourism, and culture were already crowned princes. In the Gilded Age that ended the 19th century, wealthy men collected great estates and built luxury palaces, known as "cottages," some 75 in Lenox and Stockbridge. Major literary figures toured the county: Emerson, Melville, Hawthorne, Holmes, Thoreau, Wharton, Twain. . . . Some settled here. Actors, musicians and artists followed, and are still following.

As the county now, somewhat painfully, recognizes that industries will never again be what they were through World War II, it is coming to rely on a service economy to which, at least, it is no stranger. Filled with fine educational institutions, public and private, with museums and musicians, with art and artifacts to grace the green walls installed infinitely earlier by nature, Berkshire's streams are cleaner and woods thicker than since farms and industry first came to these garrison hills. And the hills retain a plentiful supply of ground water, likely to become increasingly important to the future of this area.

Berkshire has now, as it has had since the ice left, an indigenous population that cares deeply for the land, witness the many towns in the county that have long had zoning, have now established land trusts and are considering land use countywide. Berkshire residents listen attentively at town meetings to discussions of protecting ridges and aquifers, saving farm land, and cleaning up hazardous waste. Little litter mars the many paths. Whether driving its roads or walking its trails, you will soon get the message that this land is cared for.

SOUTH COUNTY

From Gt. Barrington South: Rambling and Rolling

The section of Berkshire County from Gt. Barrington south has its own distinct rural flavor, one that has remained virtually unchanged since the land was first settled in the 18th and 19th centuries. While the rest of the county is known for its landscape and cultural events that attract thousands of visitors, the southern section is more subtle, its tranquility awaiting individual discovery.

The region east of Rte. 7 remains largely unknown to tourists, primarily because of the absence of main roads between major destinations. Instead, miles of small roads weave their way through the countryside, connecting village to village. Roughly half of them are paved, the other half dirt. All are lightly traveled, since they support primarily local traffic.

The scenery varies between knobby mountains, rolling hills and small valleys punctuated by brooks, to a gradual flattening out near the Massachusetts–Connecticut border. Each road has stretches of woodland, relieved by dozens of small farms where cows, horses, goats and sheep graze, undisturbed by the occasional traveler. Most of the rides afford sweeping views of either one or both of the larger mountains in the region, the craggy 1,649-ft. Monument Mtn., or the softer 2,624-ft. Mt. Everett, the second highest peak in the Berkshires.

The general stores located variously at Monterey, Lake Buel, Southfield, Mill River and No. Egremont constitute one of the real delights of the area. All have the authenticity of age, having served local customers for most of the last century, if not more. They stock the expected staples of groceries, hardware, doughnuts, coffee and sandwiches, as well as the latest videotapes and the morning edition of *The Wall Street*

Journal. Many have surprise items reflecting a local craft or specialty.

The South County rides also boast many classic country inns, among which are the Weathervane and Egremont inns, the Williamsville Inn between West Stockbridge and Gt. Barrington, and the Old Inn on the Green in New Marlborough.

Other offerings include the Buggy Whip Factory in Southfield, a restored wooden mill filled with establishments offering upscale selections of clothing, antiques, art and home furnishings, as well as a cafe. Antiques lovers may never leave Sheffield and So. Egremont, with their nearly two dozen antique shops.

Historical spots include the last battleground of Shays' Rebellion, a bloody uprising that followed the American Revolution and influenced the writing of the U.S. Constitution; and the American Revolution trail of General Henry Knox, roughly along Rtes. 71 and 23.

The rides start in Gt. Barrington, either at the tourist booth at the south end of town or the K-Mart/Price Chopper Plaza on the north end. Gt. Barrington is the principal commercial town in the region for good reason: the Housatonic River that flows through its center provided power for the cluster of mills that shaped the community in the 19th century.

Ride 1: *Sheffield Swing-Around*
20.3 miles; shorter version, 16.3 miles

In many respects this ride is a trip into yesterday as it meanders up and downhill through some less well-known Berkshire County landscape. Riders won't experience the manicured lawns of Lenox or Stockbridge, the sophisticated appearance of Williamstown or the country estates of Richmond. Instead they'll be treated to countryside without pretension, the two classic villages of Mill River and Southfield, and, near the end, sweeping views of Mt. Everett.

The ride has a shorter version that bypasses Southfield and the Buggy Whip Factory, substituting a visit to Umpachene Falls, hardly a spectacular waterfall but certainly a pleasant place for a picnic lunch.

The longer version goes by the Buggy Whip Factory, an unusual restoration of an old wooden mill into a complex of upscale establishments selling sweaters, clothing, tapes and music, books, antiques, art, and household furnishings. The offerings also include a cafe and pond, complete with goldfish and ducks. A visit represents the second lunch option of the trip.

The ride begins almost in the middle of Sheffield, at Rte. 7 and its intersection with Maple Ave., an inviting tree-lined residential street.

Head E. along Maple Ave., leaving the Orchard Shade guest house on the right, an establishment that has provided bed and breakfasts since 1888. As the residential area is left behind, Maple St. bears left and then crosses the Housatonic River on a new bridge that replaced the former covered bridge.

Just beyond the river is an intersection, County Rd. to the left and Hewins St. to the right. Follow County Rd. and begin to climb gradually, making sure to bear right at its intersection with Home Rd., almost 1 mi. beyond the river. For the first part of the climb the road generally follows the course of Ironworks Brook that flows into the Housatonic from Three Mile Pond, which is off to the left but not visible from the road.

The section of the ride on County Rd. is 4.7 mi., mostly uphill. It ends at a scenic little intersection with the Mill River–Gt. Barrington Rd. where the roads surround a small triangle of trees and grass. If it's picnic time, there's a good spot just across the Mill River–Gt. Barrington Rd. where an opening leads into a field.

Go right at the intersection and follow the road to Mill River, a mostly downhill ride of 1.7 mi. through fields. Mill River, among other amenities, boasts a general store and a library. And as do most others in the county, the Mill River General Store offers a generous selection of take-out sandwiches and beverages, as well as a variety of other treasures that make it well worth the stop.

From Mill River riders can choose the shorter route, which leads directly to the hamlet of Konkapot, or the longer route (by 4 mi.) that arrives at the same place but takes riders through Southfield and the Buggy Whip Factory.

For the shorter route, take the right heading out of Mill River, crossing its namesake river, and then go almost immediately left on Clayton Rd. Umpachene Falls is 1.3 mi. up the road on the left. Look for a road bearing the name of the falls, cross the river, see the falls and then visit a little picnic park just beyond the bridge on the right. To continue to Konkapot, take a left upon re-entry to Clayton Rd. and follow it gradually uphill to an intersection at a triangle green. That intersection is the approximate location of Konkapot, named for an Indian chief who, during the 1700s, sold most of southern Berkshire County to white settlers for 460 English pounds sterling, 3 barrels of cider and 30 quarts of rum.

The longer version of the ride requires taking a left turn out of Mill River on the Mill River–Southfield Rd., then climbing a hill to an intersection with Lumbert Rd. Make a left, staying on the Mill River–Southfield Rd. and climbing for another 0.5 mi. or so before the road levels off and heads downhill to a stop sign. Take a right over an iron bridge into the village of Southfield. To the right, after the bridge, is the Southfield General Store; on the left, just beyond, is the Buggy Whip Factory with its eclectic collection of shops.

Continue the ride by taking a left at the exit from the Buggy Whip, and then almost immediately go right on the Canaan–Southfield Rd., following the sign to Canaan, Connecticut. The ride heads downhill. Keep going straight, resisting the opportunity to go right at Lumbert Rd. There's an iron bridge on the right another 0.5 mi. or so along, but keep going straight. In another 1 mi., which includes well-crafted stone walls as part of the scenery, look for Konkapot Rd. on the right. Take a right at Konkapot Rd., coast down a 0.75-mi. hill to the triangle intersection with Clayton Rd., coming in from the right.

The ride is now at Konkapot where the long and short versions converge. Follow the road for 1 mi. S. through the small village; then take a right at Upton Corner Rd. Riders missing this turn will arrive in Connecticut in another 1 mi. or so.

Follow Upton Corner Rd. over Alum Hill for 1.4 mi. to a stop sign, where it intersects with Hewins St. At the top of Alum Hill the first of many panoramic views of Mt. Everett appears. Go down the other side to the intersection of Hewins St., turn right and head N., a nice easy 2.9-mi. meander with many views of Mt. Everett, back to County Rd., almost where the ride began. Take a left and head back to Sheffield, a flat trip of 1 mi.

Summary: Ride 1

0.0   Start at Maple St., Sheffield.

0.8   Bridge over Housatonic.

0.9   County Rd.–Hewins St. intersection. Bear left on County Rd.

5.6   Go right at triangle intersection with Mill River–Gt. Barrington Rd.

7.3   Mill River General Store.

Short Version

7.3   From Mill River General Store, go right, then left on Clayton Rd.

8.6   Umpachene Falls

10.1   Go right at triangle intersection with Konkapot Rd.

11.1   Go right on Upton Corner Rd. over Alum Hill.

12.5   Go right on Hewins St.

15.4   Go left at Hewins St.–County Rd. intersection to Sheffield.

16.3   Total mileage.

Long Version

7.3	From Mill River General Store go left on Mill River–Southfield Rd.
8.3	Go left on Mill River–Southfield Rd.
9.4	Go right to Southfield. Cross iron bridge.
10.0	The Buggy Whip Factory. Go left from exit and take an almost immediate right on Canaan–Southfield Rd.
13.3	Go right on Konkapot Rd.
14.1	Triangle intersection with Clayton Rd. Go straight.
15.1	Go right on Upton Corner Rd. over Alum Hill.
16.5	Go right on Hewins St.
19.4	Go left at Hewins St.–County Rd. intersection to Sheffield.
20.3	Total mileage.

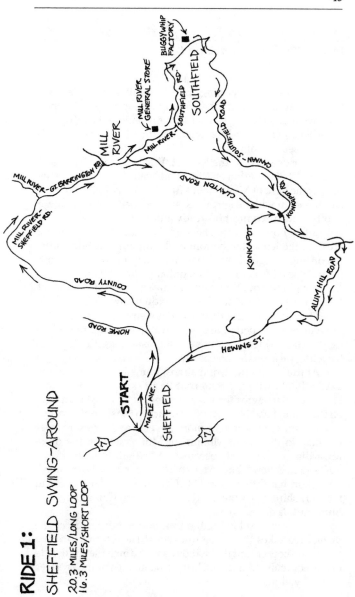

RIDE 1:
SHEFFIELD SWING-AROUND

20.3 MILES/LONG LOOP
16.3 MILES/SHORT LOOP

Ride 2: *Gt. Barrington Short Loop*
11.1 miles

This ride offers one long gradual uphill from Gt. Barrington to Monument Mtn., then a long rolling road with open rural vistas, including the well-kept grounds of the Edward J. Madden Open Heart Memorial, and finally, a 0.5-mi. moderately steep downhill going past the Butternut Basin Ski Area.

The ride starts at the K-Mart/Price Chopper Plaza just north of Gt. Barrington on Rte. 7 and heads N. on Rte. 7 to the pass at the base of Monument Mtn., a distance of 2.8 mi. The climb is even with no surprises, and the road is wide enough to offset the discomfort of steady automobile traffic.

A few hundred yards beyond the road's crest is a picnic area, on the left at the bottom of the Monument Mtn. cliffs. According to legend, an Indian maiden jumped to her death from those cliffs because of an unhappy love affair.

Roughly 0.1 mi. N. of the picnic area go right on Monument Valley Rd. for a delightful 4.6-mi. gradual downhill to Rte. 23.

The views are superb, the road is well-paved and the ride The views are superb, the road is well-paved and the ride is easy. Many riders rate this stretch as among the tops for bicycling pleasure in the county.

At Rte. 23, go right, and almost immediately head down a 0.5-mi. hill, with the Butternut Basin ski area on your left, back to Gt. Barrington for a total distance of 3.1 mi. Make a right on Rte. 7 and head N. on Rte. 7 to return to the shopping plaza.

For those in search of more adventure — or exercise — the hike to the top of Monument Mtn. is among the more rewarding in the county because the 1,649-ft. summit affords a 360-degree view from dozens of rocky perches. To the north is Stockbridge, Pittsfield and Mt. Greylock, the highest peak in the Berkshires. To the south and east are Catamount and Butternut Basin ski areas.

The ascent, following the trail on the north side of the picnic area, takes 45 minutes to an hour. The return trip can be taken on another trail that winds its way down the south side of the mountain. Monument Mtn. is maintained by the Trustees of Reservations.

RIDE 2:

GREAT BARRINGTON SHORT LOOP

11.1 MILES

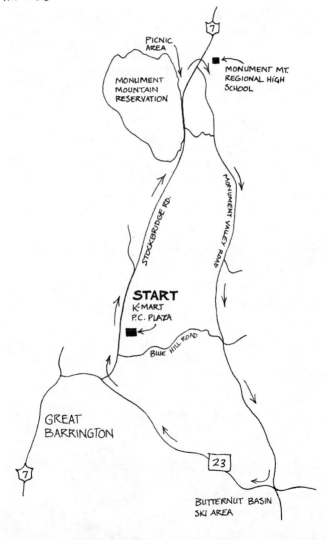

Summary: Ride 2

0.0   Start at K-Mart/Price Chopper Plaza and head N. on Rte. 7.

2.8   Go right on Monument Valley Rd. and follow S. 4.6 mi. to Rte. 23.

7.4   Go right on Rte. 23, 3.1 mi. back to Gt. Barrington, going down 0.5-mi. hill by Butternut Basin ski area.

10.5   Go right on Rte. 7, head N. to K-Mart/Price Chopper Plaza.

11.1   Total mileage.

Ride 3: *Gt. Barrington Double Loop*
23.7 miles

The double loop south of Gt. Barrington would be hard to beat for the sheer number and interest of attractions. For history buffs the ride passes by the last battle of Shays' Rebellion, a bloody skirmish in February 1787, fought over the principles of liberty and self-expression. Despite the defeat of the rebels, many historians believe their convictions shaped the writing of the U.S. Constitution the following summer in Philadelphia.

In No. Egremont a marker points to the route Gen. Henry Knox took during the American Revolution, delivering cannon from Fort Ticonderoga in New York over to Gen. George Washington, who was then engaged in driving the British from Cambridge near Boston. On Rte. 23, just south of Great Barrington near the end of the trip, the ride passes a statue commemorating the role of American newsboys in the dissemination of information.

Riders who like antiques may never reach the end of the trip. There are dozens of shops along the way, with particular concentrations in Sheffield and So. Egremont.

For animal buffs, there's a llama and alpaca farm; outdoor enthusiasts can spend the rest of their vacation money at Kenver Ltd. in So. Egremont. And finally, bicyclists who just want to get out on the road and ride will find generally flat terrain, with the exception of a couple of good workout hills at the start, and scenery that changes constantly from woods to fields to mountains.

The ride begins on Rte. 7 at the Southern Berkshire Chamber of Commerce tourist booth, just south of the business district. Start on Alford Rd., a hill that climbs for 0.8 mi. In another 1 mi., downhill, Hurlburt Rd. comes in at the left. Keep riding straight, passing Simon's Rock College of Bard's main entrance on the right and its arts center, a converted barn and a collection of red buildings, on the left. In a few hundred yards, Seekonk Rd. goes off at a shallow angle to the left. The angle is actually the hypotenuse of about a half-acre triangle intersection.

Follow Seekonk past its intersection with Division St., then up a short steep hill to Boice Rd. at the top. The craggy profile of Monument Mtn. is at the right; on the left, fields and hills.

Go left on Boice, a 1.6 mi. mostly downhill coast to its intersection with Rte. 71. Cross the road for the Gen. Henry Knox marker and the Old Egremont Store with its delicatessen and sandwich offerings, a good spot to buy take-outs for a picnic.

Head S. on Rte. 71, towards So. Egremont (go right as you leave the store, or left as you come into 71 from Boice Rd.), following the delightfully flat road through village surroundings for 1.2 mi. to where Creamery Rd. veers off to the right. If you ride by the Gt. Barrington Airport on the left, you've gone too far.

Creamery Rd. is an easy 1.6 mi. stretch to its intersection with Rte. 23, where a right leads to the village of So. Egremont. Since its attractions can be visited on the return trip, take an almost immediate left at Button Ball Lane that ends very quickly at the Egremont Inn, another choice for lunch either on the outbound trip or on the return leg.

From the inn keep heading S. on the Sheffield-Egremont Rd., a flat ride. Ivory Pond Farm, a private breeding establishment for llamas and alpacas, is on the right, about 0.5 mi. south of the inn. (The owners ask that you not feed their animals.) In another 0.5 mi., on the left, watch for the upright stone monument about 4 feet tall, marking the Shays' Rebellion final battle. Another 2 mi., through sections that afford views of Mt. Everett to the right, leads to an intersection with Rte. 7, just north of Sheffield.

About 0.25 mi. down Rte. 7 a sign at Cook Rd. on the right once pointed to the oldest covered bridge in Massachusetts, across Rte. 7 and on the left. Since a disastrous fire destroyed the 1837 structure, it can no longer be seen. There is discussion of building another covered bridge on the site, using traditional materials and building methods.

The ride then continues S. on Rte. 7, a section marked by antique shops on both sides, into the village of Sheffield, where a right is made on Berkshire School Rd., a nearly 3-mi. flat ride to Rte. 41.

From Berkshire School Rd. the ride heads N. on Rte. 41, again mostly flat, with the Berkshire School campus almost immediately on the left. The road meets Rte. 23 nearly 4 mi. north of the school, and the ride then bears right on 23 to So. Egremont, more antique shops, several inns and restaurants, and Kenver Ltd., an establishment known for ski and hiking equipment and clothing.

The ride continues along Rte. 23 to Gt. Barrington, an open stretch. The newsboy statue and fountain is on the right in its own little mini-park at the outskirts of Gt. Barrington. Built by William L. Brown, then part owner of the *New York Daily News*, as a lasting monument to news carriers everywhere, it was unveiled in October 1895 and is believed to be the oldest statue of a newsboy in the world.

Rte. 23 continues for another 0.5 mi., where it intersects with Rte. 7. Turn left for the finish at the tourist booth, another 0.2 mi.

Summary: Ride 3

0.0   Start at the Gt. Barrington tourist booth and head up the
      Alford Rd. Hill.
2.1   Go left on Seekonk Rd. that angles off obliquely.
3.5   Go left on Boice Rd. at top of hill.
5.1   Go left on Rte. 71 in front of Egremont Store.
6.3   Go right on Creamery Rd.
7.9   Go right on Rte. 23, then almost immediately left to
      Button Ball Lane and 1880 Egremont Inn.
8.2   Follow Sheffield–Egremont Rd. S.
11.7 Go right at intersection with Rte. 7.
13.4 Go right on Berkshire School Rd.
16.1 Go right on Rte. 41.
19.8 Go right on Rte. 23.
23.5 Go left on Rte. 7 for 0.2 mi. to tourist booth.
23.7 Total mileage.

RIDE 3:

GREAT BARRINGTON DOUBLE LOOP

23.7 MILES

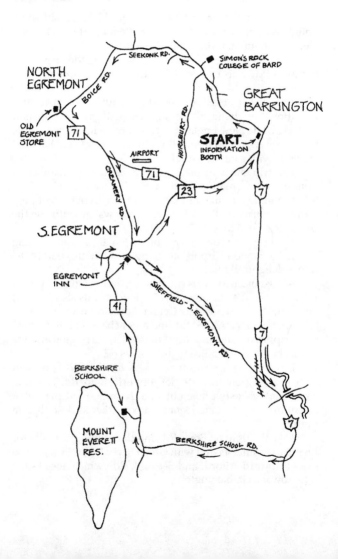

Ride 4: *Gt. Barrington–No. Egremont Loops*
Short, 6.2 miles; medium, 10 miles; long, 13.1 miles

This ride is flat for the first half, then adds spice with some uphill and a downhill at the end. It offers a particularly good view of Monument Mtn. from the south.

The trip can be shortened by taking a side trip along Hurlburt Rd. This cuts the trip's distance by approximately half.

The trip can also be extended by about 3.5 mi. by including Alford, an idyllic village complete with schoolhouse and a classic white New England-style church with a comfortable lawn for a stop. And from Alford the trip back to Gt. Barrington ends with a big downhill.

The trip starts at the Southern Berkshire Chamber of Commerce Information Booth on Rte. 7. Head S. on Rte. 7 for 0.2 mi. and then right on Rte. 23 for 1.8 mi., perhaps stopping about 0.5 mi. along Rte. 23 to visit the newsboy statue on the left as described in Ride 3.

Turn right on Rte. 71 for 3 mi. to No. Egremont, passing the Gt. Barrington Airport on the right. All of this part of the ride is delightfully flat.

If the shortened trip is your choice, the turnoff to Hurlburt Rd. is a right, 0.2 mi. along Rte. 71. Hurlburt Rd. is 1.7 uphill mi. to the Albert Schweitzer Center, now closed, then another 0.5 mi. or so to the Alford Rd. and a right back and then down for an approximate 1-mi. descent into Gt. Barrington and the tourist booth. Total mileage this way is 6.2.

If the trip is not shortened, look for the Old Egremont Store in No. Egremont on the left, opposite Boice Rd. The store has delicatessen-style take-out food. Near the road, in front of its entrance, is the Gen. Henry Knox marker as described in Ride 3.

Take the right on Boice Rd. and then climb gradually for 1.6 mi. to its intersection with Green River Rd., which goes to the left toward Alford, and Seekonk Rd., which goes to the right toward Gt. Barrington.

Here the trip can be extended for about 3.5 mi. To do so, take the left along Green River Rd. to Alford for 0.8 mi., then go right on the Alford–No. Egremont Rd. Climb gradually uphill for 1.4 mi., passing the Alford Fire Department building on the left and arriving at a triangle intersection with a sign to Alford Center, pointing right. The center of the village — the schoolhouse and the church, both on the left — is almost immediately visible.

Keep bearing right on Alford Rd. for the 4.3 mi. ride back to Gt. Barrington. One word of caution: bear left at the fork just out of the village on Alford Rd. toward Gt. Barrington. Barrington Rd., not to be taken, goes up the hill to the right. Total mileage: 13.1.

If the shorter route that would bypass Alford is preferred, head right on Seekonk Rd. at the top of the hill, where it intersects with Boice. It's mostly downhill for 1.3 mi. on Seekonk Rd., then uphill for about 0.75 mi. on Alford Rd. and then 1 mi. downhill to the tourist booth. Along Seekonk Rd. there are great views of the southern profile of Monument Mtn.

Whether the longer or the shorter version is taken, consider a visit to the campus of Simon's Rock College of Bard on Alford Rd., on the stretch between Seekonk Rd. and Hurlburt Rd. The college has a library, some ponds and, depending on the season, there may also be some soccer or baseball. There may also be an art exhibit in the arts center located in the red buildings and a converted barn across from the campus entrance.

Summary: Ride 4

0.0   Southern Berkshire Chamber of Commerce Information Booth S. on Rte. 7 for 0.2 mile to Rte. 23.

0.2   Go right on Rte. 23 for 1.8 mi.

2.0   Go right on Rte. 71 for 3 mi. to No. Egremont. Shorten the ride at this point by going right on Hurlburt Rd. 0.2 mi. along Rte. 71. Climb Hurlburt Rd., a gradual uphill for 2.3 mi., then go right on Alford Rd. for another 1.7 mi. back to the information booth.

6.2   Total mileage.

5.0   At No. Egremont, go right on Boice Rd. for 1.6 mi.
      to intersection with Green River Rd., which goes
      left to Alford, and Seekonk Rd., which goes right to
      Gt. Barrington.

6.6   Lengthen route 3.5 mi. by going left to Alford 0.8 mi.
      on Green River Rd., then right on Alford-No.
      Egremont Rd. for 1.4 mi. to sign to Alford Center,
      pointing right. Go right, taking Alford Rd. 4.3 mi.
      back to Gt. Barrington. Bear left at fork just out of
      village. Total mileage: 13.1.

6.6   Shorten route by going right on Seekonk Rd. for 1.3
      mi. to intersection with Alford Rd.

7.9   Go right on Alford Rd. for 2.1 mi. back to tourist
      booth.

10.0 Total mileage.

GREAT BARRINGTON— NORTH EGREMONT LOOP

6.2 MILES / SHORT LOOP
10 MILES / MEDIUM LOOP
13.1 MILES / LONG LOOP

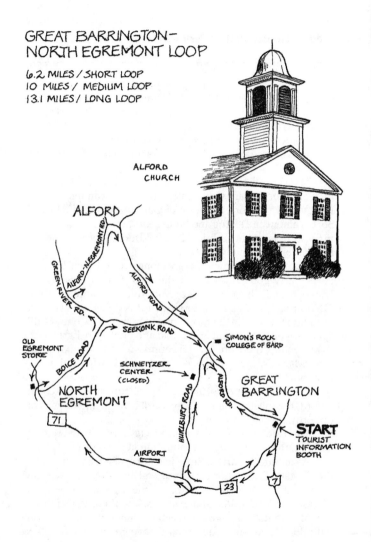

ALFORD CHURCH

ALFORD

GREEN RIVER RD.

ALFORD-N.EGREMONT RD.

ALFORD ROAD

SEEKONK ROAD

OLD EGREMONT STORE

BOICE ROAD

SIMON'S ROCK COLLEGE OF BARD

SCHWEITZER CENTER (CLOSED)

GREAT BARRINGTON

ALFORD RD.

NORTH EGREMONT

71

HURLBURT ROAD

AIRPORT

START
TOURIST INFORMATION BOOTH

23

7

Ride 5: *Gt. Barrington Perimeter Ride*
46.8 miles

A day-long odyssey along the perimeter of Rides 1-4, this trip has a little of everything, including mostly rolling terrain with a few long hills and, on occasion, some tough short ones. However, there are no real mountains.

The trip also offers several bailouts for the faint of heart, who understandably might want to shorten the distance on a hot day.

The ride abounds in shopping experiences, if time permits and pockets are sufficiently deep. They can include the Buggy Whip Factory in Southfield, antiques in Sheffield and So. Egremont and skiing and hiking equipment at Kenver Ltd. in So. Egremont. In addition, Sheffield, So. Egremont and Gt. Barrington offer many other stores.

Appropriate picnic spots are along every stretch, but two particularly good ones are at the Lake Buel access and at Umpachene Falls (just south of Mill River on an inner loop). There are at least 3 general stores with atmospheres that reflect decades of service to their local rural communities, one at Mill River (a side trip), one at Southfield and one at No. Egremont. Additionally, there are several country inns to be enjoyed, at New Marlborough, on Rte. 41 (again a side trip) and at So. Egremont.

For photographers there's the picturesque church in Alford, the meeting hall in New Marlborough and dozens of opportunities in between.

The ride also offers sweeping views of Mt. Everett, at 2,624 ft., the second-highest mountain in the Berkshires.

As in Ride 2, start on Rte. 7 just north of Gt. Barrington at the K-Mart/Price Chopper Plaza and head N. up the long gradual hill to Monument Mtn. At the top make a right on Monument Valley Rd. and pedal easily along the gradual downhill to Rte. 23, a 4.6 mile section. But at the intersection with Rte. 23, go left. Ride 2 would have gone right.

Follow Rte. 23 east, a main route with wide shoulders for the first 0.75 mi. that has not been described previously. In 1.2

mi., Rte. 57 angles in at the right. Follow Rte. 57 and head toward New Marlborough. Access to Lake Buel is on the right, 0.7 mi. from the intersection of Rtes. 23 and 57. It's a good spot for a rest stop, complete with boat ramp, picnic tables and trash cans.

After leaving the Lake Buel access, continue SE on Rte. 57 for another 1.7 mi. and the little village of Hartsville, where the ride continues straight for another 3.2 mi. (a climb with good views, big houses and old barns) to New Marlborough, which is dominated by the New Marlborough Meeting House, built in 1839, on top of the hill. The ample lawn in front of the classic building also makes a good resting spot, and a nearby monument with plaque describes the life of Elihu Burritt, 1810-1879, "the learned blacksmith," author of *The Congress of Nations* and advocate of low-rate ocean postage. Also presiding at the village setting is the historic Old Inn On The Green, established in 1739 as a hostelry that has since boasted "a welcome retreat for the world-weary traveler."

Almost opposite the meeting house is the New Marlborough–Southfield Rd., a sharp right from Rte. 57. Coast down a hill with woods on each side, past the Kolburne School on the right, for 1.3 mi. At the left is the road to Southfield with an iron bridge crossing the Umpachene Brook clearly visible.

At this point pick up the longer version of Ride 1, or continue straight to Mill River for the shorter version of Ride 1. The mileages are shown in the ride summary.

(If the Mill River option is chosen, continue to go straight for 1.1 mi.; then turn right and head toward Mill River, another 1 mi. That will join Ride 1 at the Mill River General Store.)

(There's a second possibility for shortening the ride. Head N. out of Mill River on the Gt. Barrington–Mill River Rd., a 6.1-mi. ride to Rte. 23, opposite the Monument Valley Rd. Bear right at the first choice, about 1.7 mi. out of Mill River, then bear left at the second choice, another 1.5 mi. or so. When the road reaches its intersection with Rte. 23, go left, for an approximate 3-mi. coast back to Gt. Barrington, passing the Butternut Basin ski area on the left. At Rte. 7 take a right for less than a mile to the K-Mart/Price Chopper Plaza and the start-finish for the trip.)

To return to the perimeter ride, cross the bridge as in Ride 1. The Southfield General Store is on the right, and just beyond on the left is the Buggy Whip Factory, another possibility for lunch, either picnic-style, with take-out food available on the premises, or in the Factory's Cafe.

Continue by taking a left at the exit from the Buggy Whip, and then almost immediately go right on the Canaan–Southfield Rd., following the sign to Canaan, CT. The ride heads downhill. Keep going straight, resisting the opportunity to go right at Lumbert Rd. There's an iron-railed bridge on the right another mile or so along, but keep going straight. In another mile, past well-crafted stone walls, look for Konkapot Rd., which comes in from the right. Take a right at Konkapot Rd. and coast down a 0.75-mi. hill to the triangle intersection with Clayton Rd., coming in from the right.

The ride is now at Konkapot, where the long and short versions of Ride 1 converge. Follow the road S. through the small village, and in about 1 mi. take a right at Upton Corner Rd. Riders missing this turn will arrive in Connecticut in another mile or so.

Follow Upton Corner Rd. over Alum Hill for 1.4 mi., to a stop sign where it intersects with Hewins St. At the top of Alum Hill the first of many panoramic views of Mt. Everett appears. Go down the other side to the intersection of Hewins St., make a right and head N., a nice easy 3-mi. meander with many views of Mt. Everett. Hewins intersects with County Rd. in a "yield" situation. Bear left, cross the bridge over the Housatonic and pedal along Maple St. to Sheffield and Rte. 7, a flat 1-mi. stretch.

At Sheffield the ride can again be shortened by heading N. for about a mile on Rte. 7, then bearing left on the Sheffield–Egremont Rd. for 3.5 mi. to So. Egremont, a generally flat ride that goes by the Shays' Rebellion battlefield. At So. Egremont, go right on Rte. 23 for the 3.4-mi. trip back to Gt. Barrington. This route is part of Ride 3 but in reverse.

If the longer version is chosen, go left on Rte. 7 for 0.5 mi. through the village of Sheffield, then right on Berkshire School Rd. for 2.8 mi. until its intersection with Rte. 41. Sheffield offers a choice of stores.

At Rte. 41, head N. The Berkshire School campus is almost immediately on the left. The road meets Rte. 23 about 3.5 mi. north of the school, and the ride then bears right on Rte. 23 to So. Egremont, more antique shops, the Egremont Inn (which is off to the right of Rte. 23) and Kenver Ltd. for skiing/hiking gear.

(Again, the ride can be shortened at this point by following Rte. 23 for nearly 4 mi. back to Gt. Barrington. Follow Rte. 7, 2.1 mi. N. through downtown and N. again toward Stockbridge. The K-Mart/Price Chopper Plaza, the ride's start, will be on the right, just out of town.)

If strength is left for a few more hills, the perimeter ride continues from So. Egremont to Alford and then becomes flat, followed by a 0.75-mi. hill, then a 1-mi. downhill to Gt. Barrington.

Follow Rte. 23 out of So. Egremont to an almost immediate triangle intersection with Creamery Rd., heading straight where Rte. 23 bears right. A sign will point to Rte. 71, No. Egremont. Climb Creamery Rd. 1.6 mi. to its intersection with Rte. 71. Bear left and follow Rte. 71 for 1.3 mi. to No. Egremont, looking for the Old Egremont Store at the left, a possibility for a food and rest stop.

Take a right on Boice Rd., directly opposite the store, then climb for a little more than a mile to its intersection with Green River Rd. Go left for 0.75-mi. of flat riding, then right on the Alford-No. Egremont Rd. to the picturesque town of Alford, a postcard scene complete with church and 1-room school.

The ride can be shortened by about 3.5 mi. by turning right at the top of Boice Rd. onto Seekonk Rd. That will lead to Alford Rd., the 0.75-mi. uphill, then the 1-mi. downhill to Gt. Barrington for a left on Rte. 7 back to the K-Mart/Price Chopper Plaza.

At Alford go right on West Rd., which becomes Alford Rd. in the center of the village. Follow Alford Rd. but bear left almost immediately outside the village center and ride the 4.3-mi. trip to Gt. Barrington. The stretch is generally flat with one 0.75-mi. climb just after Hurlburt Rd. before a delightful 1-mi.

descent into Gt. Barrington.

Alford Rd. ends at Rte. 7. Take a left and head N. for 1.9 mi., through the Gt. Barrington downtown. Keep following Rte. 7 toward Stockbridge, and the K-Mart/Price Chopper Plaza, where the ride started, is on the right, just out of town.

Summary: Ride 5

0.0   Start at K-Mart/Price Chopper Plaza and go right from exit on Rte. 7 heading N. toward Stockbridge.

2.8   Go right on Monument Valley Rd.

7.4   Go left on Rte. 23.

8.6   Go right on Rte. 57.

9.3   Lake Buel access.

11.0   Hartsville.

14.2   New Marlborough. Go right on New Marlborough–Southfield Rd. opposite meeting house.

15.5   Go left to Southfield. Cross iron bridge.

Ride can be shortened at this point by continuing on New Marlborough–Southfield Rd. to Mill River, 2.1 mi. At Mill River, pick up Mill River–Gt. Barrington Rd. and follow it for 6.1 mi. to its intersection with Rte. 23. Go left on Rte. 23 to Gt. Barrington and then right on Rte. 7 to K-Mart/Price Chopper Plaza, a distance of 3.7 mi. Total distance of shorter version is 27.4 mi.

16.1   The Buggy Whip Factory. Go left from exit 0.2 mi. and take almost immediate right on Canaan–Southfield Rd.

19.4   Go right on Konkapot Rd.

20.2   Go straight at triangle intersection with Clayton Rd.

21.2   Go right on Upton Corner Rd. over Alum Hill.

22.6   Go right on Hewins St.

25.5   Go left at Hewins St.–County Rd. intersection to Sheffield.

RIDE 5:

GREAT BARRINGTON PERIMETER RIDE

46.8 MILES

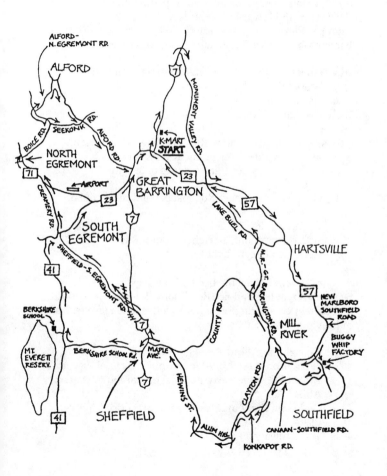

Again there is a choice for a shorter ride. Go right on
Rte. 7 for 1.2 mi. to the Sheffield–Egremont Rd. that comes
in from the left. Follow that road for 3.5 mi. to So.
Egremont and then go right on 23. Follow 23 for 3.4 mi. to
Rte. 7, then go left for 2.4 mi., through downtown Gt.
Barrington and toward Stockbridge. The K-Mart/Price
Chopper Plaza, where the ride started, is just outside Gt.
Barrington. The total distance for this version is 36 mi.

26.4   Go left on Rte. 7 for 0.5 mi., then right on Berkshire
       School Rd.
29.6   Go right on Rte. 41.
33.3   Go right on Rte. 23.

Again a choice. Follow Rte. 23 to Rte. 7, then left on
Rte. 7 as in previous description. Ride will end at K-Mart/
Price Chopper Plaza for total distance of 39.7 mi.

34.0   Go left on Creamery Rd., just beyond center of So.
       Egremont.
35.6   Go left on Rte. 71.
36.8   At No. Egremont, go right on Boice Rd.
38.4   Go left on Green River Rd.

Or, again, shorten the trip by 3.5 mi. by going right on
Seekonk Rd. at top of Boice Rd. That will lead to Alford Rd.
and then to Gt. Barrington, where a left is taken on Rte. 7 as
in previous descriptions.

39.2   Go right on Alford–No. Egremont Rd.
40.6   Go right on West Rd., which within a few yards becomes
       Alford Rd. When leaving village, bear left to stay on
       Alford Rd.
44.9   Go left on Rte. 7 and back to K-Mart/Price Chopper
       Plaza.
46.8   Total mileage.

Ride 6: *Great Josh Billings Practice Ride*
27 miles

For the handful of athletes in the world who haven't heard of The Great Josh Billings Run-Aground, Berkshire County's most famous test of endurance, it's a mid-September biking-canoeing-running race that requires serious training for all parties. The competition routinely draws more than 1,000 competitors, and although veteran observers say that it's won on the water, the bicyclists set the pace.

The Josh Billings trip is included because it's an outstanding recreational ride, even though it's not a loop. The non-loop solution is to send non-bikers in the party to the Stockbridge Bowl to prepare a picnic for the arrival of the bicyclists. Top Josh racers do the course in a little more than an hour. The rest of us take two hours or more.

The race starts on Rte. 7 at the Gt. Barrington K-Mart/Price Chopper Plaza. Go left when leaving the plaza, and head S. on Rte. 7 through downtown Gt. Barrington. After passing the Town Hall on the right, go right on the Alford Rd., and begin the 1-mi. climb that separates the packs as the race begins.

The hill levels off and then descends for 0.75 mi. as the road heads toward Alford. Just past Hurlburt Rd., the entrance to the Simon's Rock College of Bard campus is on the right.

Alford, with its classic New England church and 1-room schoolhouse, is nearly 5.5 mi. into the race. Almost immediately before those signature buildings is a triangle intersection with a sign and arrows pointing to West Rd. on the left; East Rd. on the right.

Take East Rd., bearing to the right, into a dip and over a bridge before it climbs for about 1 mi. followed by 2.5 mi. of up-and-down, with the ups slightly more than the downs. The way may be slow, but the upside of the uphills is the sweeping cross-valley views the route affords. Follow East Rd. for 4.1 mi. until the grassy intersection of East Alford Rd. and West Center Rd. At this point, the trip odometer will read 9.5 mi., give or take a tenth.

Bear left at the intersection, following West Center Rd.

(A right will take you to Rte. 41 in 1.6 mi. If you want to return to Gt. Barrington, go right on 41 and follow it to Rte. 7 in Gt. Barrington, about 6.5 mi. Go left on Rte. 7, back to the K-Mart/Price Chopper plaza.)

As a less hilly alternative to East Rd., bicyclists may want to choose the "old" Josh Billings route on West Rd. The route was changed in favor of the hillier side of the valley a few years ago to spread out the racers. The old route became too easy, with the result that bicyclists were able to ride in huge packs, which created a dangerous situation at bike-canoe handoff time at the Stockbridge Bowl. The theory — which has proved itself — was that a switch to the hillier East Rd. route would separate the very fast from the merely fast, resulting in less congestion, more safety.

To ride the "old" Josh route, bear left in the center of Alford, then right on West Rd., a long gradual uphill that provides a view to the right over a narrow valley to knobby mountains on the other side.

West Rd. heads north for approximately 5 mi. with some downhill dips near the end until it reaches the East Alford Rd.—West Center Rd. intersection, a grassy little triangle arrangement with a stop sign. This is where the newer East Rd. version of the Josh converges with the older West Rd. route.

Take a left and follow West Center Rd. N., going uphill for 2 mi. until reaching a crest, then literally flying downhill for more than a mile, watching the countryside open up until the intersection with Rte. 102, just W. of W. Stockbridge, where the course goes right.

A little more than 1 mi. on Rte. 102 takes the course towards the village of W. Stockbridge, then down a small hill and right, still following Rte. 102, this time S. to Stockbridge with a couple of hills ahead but a good road underneath. The crest is about 1.5 mi. out of W. Stockbridge, then it's downhill for another 1.5 mi. to Stockbridge and a sharp left turn at the Stockbridge clock tower, Town Hall and Congregational Church.

From there it's a flat ride for about 0.75 mi. on a wide main street flanked by large houses and trees to the Red Lion Inn, where the course takes an abrupt left around the monument

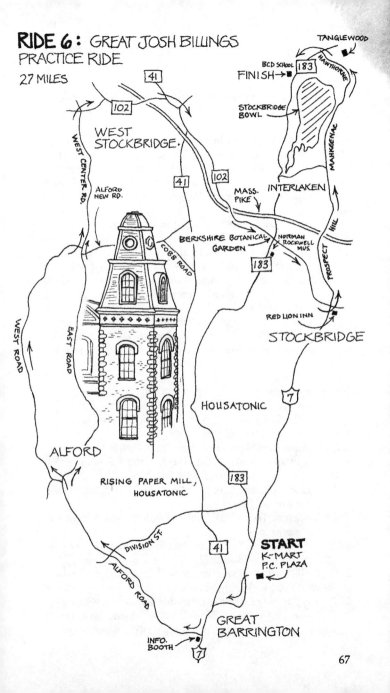

RIDE 6: GREAT JOSH BILLINGS PRACTICE RIDE

27 MILES

TANGLEWOOD

BCD SCHOOL
FINISH →
HAWTHORNE
183

STOCKBRIDGE BOWL

41

102

WEST STOCKBRIDGE

WEST CENTER RD.

ALFORD NEW RD.

41

102

MASS. PIKE

INTERLAKEN

MAHKEENAC

COBB ROAD

BERKSHIRE BOTANICAL GARDEN

NORMAN ROCKWELL MUS.

183

PROSPECT HILL

EAST ROAD

RED LION INN

STOCKBRIDGE

WEST ROAD

HOUSATONIC

7

ALFORD

RISING PAPER MILL, HOUSATONIC

183

DIVISION ST.

41

START
K-MART
P.C. PLAZA

ALFORD ROAD

INFO. BOOTH

GREAT BARRINGTON

7

and heads up Pine St., past St. Paul's Church on the right and curving left uphill to Prospect Hill Rd. after the tennis courts on the left.

Prospect Hill is a 2-miler, with some flat sections for relief. The course goes past former estates on the left and right, then the Stockbridge town beach on the left (open to residents and guests only). It hugs a cove in the Stockbridge Bowl, then heads uphill for 0.5 mi. before flattening out on a stretch before Rte. 183.

The race, now in its final leg, passes the huge hedge denoting the south side of Tanglewood on the right, then takes a sharp left on Rte. 183 for the final downhill mile to the finish.

On race day, the finish, at the entrance to the public access for the Bowl, is a place for pandemonium as the tightly packed bicyclists hurtle in and then frantically look for their canoeists to hand off a wrist band.

Otherwise, it's all quite placid. End the trip at the access to the Bowl and join the picnic. If riders do it early enough on a Sunday during the summer, they can catch the afternoon concert at Tanglewood.

Summary: Ride 6

0.0   Leave K-Mart/Price Chopper Plaza and head S. on
           Rte. 7, through Gt. Barrington downtown.
1.3   Go right on Alford Rd.
5.4   Alford. Bear rightfollowing sign to East Rd.
9.5   Go left at East Alford Rd.–West Center Rd. intersection
12.8   Go right at intersection with Rte. 102.
14.1   Follow 102 through center of W. Stockbridge and then
           right toward Stockbridge.
17.5   Go left at Town Hall/clock tower/church complex in
           Stockbridge.
19.4   Go left on Pine St. up Prospect Hill in front of Red Lion
           Inn, almost in Stockbridge Center.
24.9   Go left on Rte. 183 for final downhill mile to finish at boat
           access to Stockbridge Bowl.
25.7   Total mileage. That's the author's mileage. Officially,
           however, the race is 27 mi. The discrepancy just proves
           the point about odometers. They never agree.

Ride 7: *Gt. Barrington–W. Stockbridge Loop*
28.5 miles

This ride offers a gradual climb from Gt. Barrington to W. Stockbridge, a town experiencing an interesting rebirth, and then a return route along the western border of the county through the town of Alford, a way offering unusually beautiful views of farmland.

Both towns are interesting for different reasons. Until the early 1970s, W. Stockbridge's history was primarily influenced by its location as a gateway to the western central part of the county because of the Hudson and Berkshire Railroad, whose way was laid out in 1838.

The Williams River, which runs through the town, became a source of power for grist mills in the early days of the village, stimulating commerce. Augmenting the mills were the quarrying operations that took place in the surrounding hills.

In 1973 a New York developer bought most of the old business buildings between Main St. and the river and then refurbished them for rental to craftspeople in a major effort to transform the town into a center for selling craftwork. The effort has had its ups and downs, with the realization of the original dream not yet fulfilled. Still, W. Stockbridge has gems, including some notable restaurants as well as antique and boutique establishments.

Alford, about 10 mi. south of W. Stockbridge, is a classic New England village with its well-defined center of a church, town hall, schoolhouse and residences. The open agricultural area surrounding the town stands as testimony to the value of farmland for scenery, since it's reported that about 60 percent of the land in the town is owned by New Yorkers.

The ride starts at the K-Mart/Price Chopper Plaza on Rte. 7 just north of Gt. Barrington and proceeds S. on Rte. 7 for 1.2 mi. to its intersection with Rte. 41, where it makes a sharp right, leaving Rte. 7 and heading N. on Rte. 41, first climbing a hill and then opening out onto a flat section with pretty views on both sides.

The ride continues through the little village of Williams-ville, with a rest stop recommended at the Williamsville Inn, one of the county's older country-lodging places. Located at the foot of Tom Ball Mtn., the main house was built in 1797.

Climb the 0.5 mi. from Williamsville and then proceed along the very gradual uphill to W. Stockbridge, a total of about 11 mi. from the ride's start. The roads from W. Stockbridge south then thread their way through magnificent farm scenery.

Make a left on Rte. 102 in W. Stockbridge, heading W. on Main St., then make another left at its end, crossing the river and passing the Shaker Mill, an antiques place, on the left. Continue on Rte. 102 past where Rte. 41 bears off to the right, go over the Mass. Pike and then go left on Center Rd., 1.9 mi. from W. Stockbridge center.

Follow this road for 3.3 mi. to a triangle intersection where the ride goes right on West Rd. and 4.9 mi., mostly downhill, to the center of Alford. There's a nice choice at the West Center Rd.– East Alford Rd. triangle intersection. Go straight on East Alford Rd., which follows the east side of the valley, a 4-mi. gradual downhill to Alford.

Whichever way Alford is approached, keep bearing left with the objective of connecting to the Alford Rd. and Gt. Barrington. Immediately outside the village on the Alford Rd. bear left on the main road, even though the Barrington Rd. tempts riders to go straight.

Alford Rd. heads gradually downhill for 2.6 mi. to Hurlburt Rd. on the right, passing Simon's Rock College of Bard on the left. Remain on Alford Rd. past the Hurlburt turnoff, going first uphill for 0.75 mi. and then down for approximately 1 mi. to the intersection with Rte. 7 at the Gt. Barrington information booth.

Turn left on Rte. 7, go through the Gt. Barrington business district and follow Rte. 7 N. to the K-Mart/Price Chopper Plaza, a distance of 1.9 mi.

RIDE 7:

GREAT BARRINGTON– W. STOCKBRIDGE LOOP

28.5 MILES

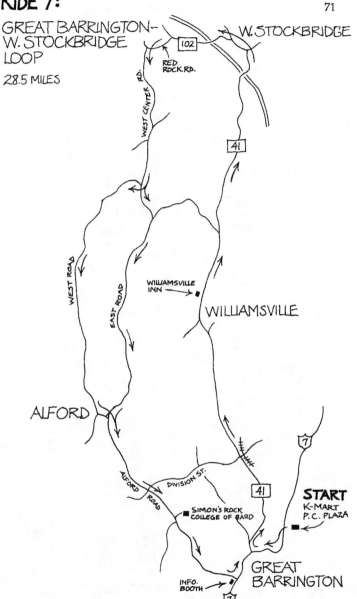

W. STOCKBRIDGE

102

RED ROCK RD.

WEST CENTER RD.

41

WEST ROAD

EAST ROAD

WILLIAMSVILLE INN

WILLIAMSVILLE

ALFORD

7

ALFORD ROAD

DIVISION ST.

41

SIMON'S ROCK COLLEGE OF BARD

START
K-MART
P.C. PLAZA

INFO. BOOTH

GREAT BARRINGTON

7

Summary: Ride 7

- 0.0 From K-Mart/Price Chopper Plaza, go S. on Rte. 7, 1.2 mi. to intersection with Rte. 41.
- 1.2 Go right, following Rte. 41 for 11 mi. to intersection with Rte. 102 in W. Stockbridge.
- 12.2 Go left on Rte. 102 following it for 1.9 mi. until left turn at Center Rd. Follow Center Rd. for 3.3 mi.
- 17.4 Go right on Alford Rd. at triangle intersection for 4.9 mi. (Or keep going straight on 0.6-mi. connector to East Rd. and then go right for 4.1 mi. to Alford.)
- 22.3 Go left at Alford for 4.3 mi. to Rte. 7 in Gt. Barrington.
- 26.6 Go left on Rte. 7 for 1.9 mi. back to start.
- 28.5 Total mileage.

Estates and Industry: Stockbridge, Lenox and Housatonic

The rides around these three communities offer a fascinating glimpse into the industrial revolution and its impact on communities during the last half of the 19th century.

The development of Stockbridge, Lenox and Housatonic provides a dramatic reflection of the social divisions created by the birth of large-scale industry in New England. At the top were mill owners and old-wealth families; at the bottom were the proud but poor who worked in the mills.

As part of the fallout from these social distinctions, Stockbridge and Lenox became watering places for the aristocracy of a gilded age. In contrast, Housatonic, thanks to the river, became the hub of thriving industry.

Before the days of mass marketing, the outside world discovered unknown areas through descriptive passages in the works of novelists and poets. And so it was with the Stockbridge–Lenox area, which drew a number of famous authors during the early- and mid-19th century. At one time or another their ranks included William Cullen Bryant, Catherine Sedgwick, Nathaniel Hawthorne, Oliver Wendell Holmes, Henry Wadsworth Longfellow, Henry Ward Beecher, Henry David Thoreau and Herman Melville.

Their writing included rapturous descriptions of Berkshire scenery, especially in the area around Stockbridge, Lenox and south of Pittsfield. At the same time, the industrial revolution in America had created huge fortunes, with the result that wealthy people, attracted by the writings of these well-known authors, began to visit the Berkshires and then establish themselves in estates around Lenox and Stockbridge.

They called their places "cottages" and designed them with careful attention so that they could take advantage of the spectacular views of Monument Mtn., the Stockbridge Bowl or other attractive features of the landscape. The estate owners also contributed their talents to improving the beauty of Stockbridge and Lenox by laying out wide streets, planting trees along them and providing for lawns between the sidewalks and roads.

In a very real sense by 1900 the Stockbridge–Lenox area had developed into a huge park, dotted with rolling lawns, ponds, imaginatively shaped trees, curving walks and carefully manicured grounds. That kind of lifestyle no longer exists, but the effects are still attractively pronounced in the Lenox–Stockbridge area, where former estates have become schools, museums, music centers, galleries or spa resorts.

The village of Housatonic has a different story, one much more directly connected to the industrial revolution and the use of water power. The Housatonic River, flowing down from Stockbridge, Lee and Pittsfield, supplied power for two major mills, Monument Mills, a cotton factory in the center of town, and what is now the Rising Paper Company just south of Housatonic. The village itself is laid out in the typical mill town pattern, with houses and businesses clustered around the river that runs between 2 mountains.

Monument Mills closed in the early 1950s, and for many years its gutted hulk served as a gloomy reminder of a better past. As of the mid-1990s, however, there are signs of a rebirth, as small businesses, some artistic in nature, plant tentative roots in the mill's cavernous spaces.

The Rising Paper Company is startling in its Victorian architecture, with 4 stories and 2 towers rising majestically behind tall spruce trees along Rte. 183 and the river flowing along its other side, coursing through a dam just above the mill. When built in 1876, the mill was the largest paper plant in the world. The company, which has occupied the mill since 1899, is now a division of Fox River Paper of Appleton, WI, and produces printing and fine arts paper.

Rte. 183 weaves its way through the history of all three towns, beginning in Housatonic and then following the river, at times rough with rapids, passing just north of the Stockbridge business district to end in Lenox, after going by Tanglewood and other estates. The road rolls with the land, seldom intruding on its natural features and allowing the rider to contemplate the 19th-century conditions that shaped the histories of these three towns.

Most of the rides start at the Red Lion Inn in Stockbridge,

a traditional country lodging place. The inn, perhaps the most famous of its kind in New England, has 108 rooms, a spacious front porch, indoor and outdoor dining, a cozy tavern, an inviting hearth and many other amenities for the traveler, whether on bicycle or otherwise.

While the Red Lion Inn is easily the most famous hostelry in New England, if not in the country, the Lenox–Stockbridge area offers a rich smorgasbord of country inns or estates made into inns. In addition, there are a number of spa-resorts or conference centers.

As for culture, nowhere else in the county, with the possible exception of Williamstown, can boast such a concentration of theater, music, art and architecture. The following list represents thumbnail sketches of major attractions in the area and the rides that include them on their routes.

Berkshire Botanical Garden, Stockbridge. (Rides 6, 8, 9, 10, 11, 13)

Located at the junction of Rtes. 102 and 183, just northwest of Stockbridge, the 15-acre center's offerings include beautiful gardens, a solar heated greenhouse, lily ponds, herbs, youth programs, exhibits, lectures, workshops and a gift shop. Picnics are invited. Open May 1 to Oct. 31, 10–5, daily. Fee.

Berkshire Theatre Festival, Stockbridge. (Ride 10)

While Ride 10 is the only one that goes directly by the Berkshire Playhouse, the home of the Berkshire Theatre Festival, at the foot of Yale Hill, the theater is only about a 10-minute walk from the Red Lion Inn. Ask anybody for directions. The festival's second theater, the Unicorn, produces contemporary American works, including premiere pieces by new playwrights. Also sponsored are staged readings and children's theater. Season is July and August.

Chesterwood, Stockbridge. (Rides 8, 9, 13)

Sculptor Daniel Chester French (1850-1931) is best known for his *Seated Lincoln* statue in the Lincoln Memorial, Washington, D.C. and his *Minute Man at Concord*. He came to Stockbridge in 1896 and for 3 decades created sculpture from a studio exactingly planned for its special function. The estate is both a National Historic Landmark and Massachusetts Historic Landmark. Its offerings include memorabilia, a gallery, and a museum shop, as well as an Italianate garden and nature walks. Open May 1–Oct. 31, 10–5 daily. Fee. Free to Chesterwood members and members of National Trust for Historic Preservation. Special events are scheduled during the season.

Edith Wharton Restoration, The Mount, Shakespeare & Co., Lenox. (Rides 10, 12, 16)

Pulitzer-Prize-winning author Edith Wharton built The Mount in 1902 on the classical precepts of her popular book, *The Decoration of Houses* (1897). In addition to *Ethan Frome* (1911), set in the Berkshires, her celebrated novels include *The House of Mirth* (1905), *The Custom of the Country* (1913) and *The Age of Innocence* (1920). The gardens, which like the mansion are being restored, were designed by the author at the same time she was writing *Italian Villas and Their Gardens* (1903).

During July and August, Shakespeare & Co. performs on the grounds, taking advantage of a natural amphitheater and the mansion's balconies. There are also plays and readings that take place inside the mansion, sponsored by Edith Wharton Restoration. Open: Memorial Day through Oct. Tour schedules vary. Call 413-637-1899 for up-to-date information.

Mission House, Stockbridge. (Rides 6, 8, 9, 10, 11)

The Mission House on Main St., Stockbridge, is the former

home of the Rev. John Sergeant, first missionary to the Stockbridge Indians. The authentic colonial furnishings reflect the separate interests of Sergeant and his wife, Abigail, providing a glimpse of the domesticity of the era. The gardens, designed by Boston landscape architect Fletcher Steele, are particularly interesting. The property is maintained by The Trustees of Reservations. Open Memorial Day weekend—Columbus Day, Tue–Sun., and Mon. holidays, 11–4 p.m. Fee. Guided tours.

The National Music Center, Lenox. (Rides 10, 12, 16)

While the National Music Center is located directly along the route for Rides 10, 12 and 16, it is also an easy connection for 11, 13, 14 and 15, because all of them either begin or skirt the Lenox Town Hall. The music center is about 1 mi. from the Town Hall. Take Walker St. for 0.2 mi., then go right on Kemble St. for nearly another mile. The music center is on the right.

Under development in 1994, the center is expected to become a major Berkshire attraction. Located on a 63-acre campus, facilities and programs will include a residence where professionals from music, radio and recording can retire and share their musical heritage with students. Also planned is an interactive museum featuring all of American music, a music library and special programs.

Naumkeag, Stockbridge. (Rides 6, 11, 12)

Naumkeag was the summer home of Joseph H. Choate, renowned late 19th-century lawyer and once ambassador to the Court of St. James. The estate provides a glimpse of the kinds of lavish surroundings that made the Stockbridge – Lenox area famous. Designed by Stanford White in 1886, the house is considered both elegant and unusual. The gardens, designed by Boston landscape architect Fletcher Steele, are particularly interesting. The property is maintained by The Trustees of Reservations. House and gardens open late May to Columbus Day, Tues.– Sun. and Mon. holidays, 10– 4:15. Fee. Guided tours.

Norman Rockwell Museum, Stockbridge. (Rides 8, 9, 10, 13)

The Norman Rockwell Museum, on the Linwood Estate on Rte. 183 just north of Stockbridge, houses the only permanent collection of Norman Rockwell paintings on public display in the United States, including many *Saturday Evening Post* covers. Rockwell, perhaps the nation's best-known illustrator, lived in Stockbridge from 1953 until his death in 1978. Formerly located in the middle of Stockbridge, where it attracted crowds way beyond its capacity for accommodation, the museum moved to new quarters in 1993, following a successful national fund drive. The new quarters have elevated the museum to a major Berkshire attraction, drawing thousands of visitors each season.

Located on Rte. 183, .06 mi. south of the junction of Rtes. 183 and 102, the museum is open year-round. From May–Oct. the hours are 10–5; from Nov.–Apr. hours are weekdays 11–4, weekends 10–5. Closed Thanksgiving, Christmas, New Year's Day. Rockwell's studio is open May–Oct. Fee. Tours.

Pleasant Valley Sanctuary, Lenox. (Ride 14)

The main entrance to the Pleasant Valley Sanctuary is off busy Rte. 7, about two miles north of Lenox center. Because of the traffic on Rte. 7, no rides are routed past the access roads to the sanctuary. However, it is reachable as a variation of Ride 14, the Lenox Meander, but only for riders who are up to the demands of a steep hill. The sanctuary has extensive nature walks, including a half-day hike up Lenox Mtn. to the firetower with panoramic views from the summit; a small trailside museum; and varieties of native plants. The sanctuary is maintained by the Massachusetts Audubon Society. Open daily, sunrise to sunset. Fee.

Tanglewood, Lenox. (Rides 6, 10, 11, 13, 14)

A lovely 210-acre estate overlooking the Stockbridge Bowl, Tanglewood has been the permanent summer home of the Boston Symphony Orchestra since 1936. Major concerts are given on Friday and Saturday evenings and Sunday afternoons during July and August, many of them under the direction of guest conductors. In addition, there are other offerings, including open rehearsals of the B.S.O. and concerts by musicians of the Tanglewood Music Center. Tanglewood draws about 300,000 visitors to its programs each summer, and as such is a major tourist offering in the Berkshires. Even without a concert, the grounds, including the new Seiji Ozawa Hall, are worth a visit. During concerts, the grounds draw hundreds of picnickers who can sit on the lawn at a reduced admission. Any bicyclist who wants to tour in and around Tanglewood on a Sunday afternoon in July and August had better be prepared for extremely heavy traffic. Call (413) 637-1940 for ticket information during the season.

Tyringham Art Gallery and **Gingerbread House,** Tyringham. (Ride 12)

Slightly off the beaten path for most tourists are the Tyringham Gallery and Gingerbread House, the former studio of Sir Henry Hudson Kitson, the sculptor who created the *Minute Man* at Lexington. The building is unusual with a roof fashioned of conventional materials to simulate thatching. Many consider the house with its rolling roof a gigantic piece of sculpture. The gallery offerings include painting, sculpture and ceramics by nationally known artists. Open Memorial Day weekend to Columbus Day, 10–5. Fee.

Ride 8: *Stockbridge–Cherry Hill Challenge*
4.3 miles; longer version to Chesterwood, 6.5 miles; or variation that passes by the Norman Rockwell Museum, 4.8 miles.

The Cherry Hill Challenge offers three choices and at the same time provides the opportunity to visit three of the county's top attractions: Chesterwood, the Norman Rockwell Museum and the Berkshire Botanical Garden.

The basic and shortest version of the ride, however, is simply a pretty meander with some short hills through some of the residential areas of Stockbridge as well as a short traverse of the Stockbridge Golf Club, and a crossing of the Housatonic River. The ride is good, either for a leisurely morning or afternoon or for a warm-up before a longer trip and the chance to adjust gears.

The ride may also be extended for 3.2 mi. with a visit to Chesterwood, home of the sculptor, Daniel Chester French in Glendale. The extension, if done as a loop, involves some riding on unpaved roads.

A variation continues north on Rte. 183, past Mohawk Lake Rd. and its access to Chesterwood, to the junction of Rtes. 183 and 102. This version goes by the Norman Rockwell Museum and the Berkshire Botanical Garden at the junction of the two numbered routes.

The ride starts at the Red Lion Inn and follows Rte. 102 W. for 0.4 mi. to the cluster of scenic buildings that includes the First Congregational Church, the Stockbridge clock tower and the Stockbridge Town Hall. Rte. 102 goes right, but this ride continues straight, through the Stockbridge Golf Club course and over the Housatonic River, bearing to the right after the bridge.

From the Housatonic, start the climb up Cherry Hill, and ride over the bridge crossing railroad tracks. In about 0.5 mi. the road goes straight over a railroad crossing. Just before the crossing, turn left on Cherry Hill Rd., climb a hill for 0.2 mi. and then coast downhill for another 0.4 mi. until a T intersection. Go left at the T, continue for another climb of about 0.4 mi., where there's a small triangle intersection. Go right, and down a hill for 0.5 mi. to the intersection of Cherry Hill Rd. with Goodrich St., marked by a teardrop shape large grassy area. Turn left on Goodrich St. and follow it for 0.5 mi. to its intersection with Rte. 7. Turn left on Rte. 7 for the 0.6 mi. trip back to the Red Lion Inn.

If the Chesterwood extension is chosen, cross the railroad

tracks and in 0.1 mi. the road meets Rte. 183 in the center of the village of Glendale. Go right for 0.2 mi., then left on Mohawk Lake Rd. Then take another left almost immediately for the 0.5-mi. ride to Chesterwood. The road, paved at first and then dirt, is marked by a directional sign to Chesterwood.

The ride can continue after Chesterwood by going right at the exit and continuing along the dirt road. At the first fork, 0.2 mi. from the entrance, bear right, going down a small hill for .4 mi. Go left at the T intersection and in another 0.5 mi. the ride joins Rte. 183. Go left for 1.1 mi. back to Glendale, then go right and pick up the shorter version at the 1.7 mi. mark, immediately after crossing railroad tracks.

The variation of the ride, the one that goes by the Norman Rockwell Museum, begins as part of the Chesterwood extension. Instead of turning left at Mohawk Lake Rd. to go to Chesterwood (Chesterwood remains as an obvious optional side trip), continue straight on Rte. 183 for 1 mi. until it reaches the intersection with Rte. 102. The Norman Rockwell Museum is on the right and the Berkshire Botanical Garden is at the intersection of Rtes. 183 and 102.

To return to Stockbridge, take Rte. 102 south for 1.5 mi., following it as it goes left at the First Congregational Church for another 0.4 mi. to the Red Lion Inn.

Summary: Ride 8

0.0   Start at Red Lion Inn and follow Rte. 102 west for 0.4 mi., where Congregational Church, clock tower and Town Hall are on left and Rte. 102 goes right.

0.4   Go straight ahead, dipping down a small hill, crossing Stockbridge golf course and bridge over Housatonic, then bearing right and going straight, taking bridge over tracks and continuing to rail crossing.

1.7   Go left on Cherry Hill Rd. before crossing tracks, climb hill for 0.2 mi., then go downhill for 0.4 mi. until a T intersection.

2.3   Go left at T intersection for 0.4 mi. up hill.

2.7   At top of hill go right at little triangle, then downhill for 0.5 mi. to Goodrich St.

3.2   Go left on Goodrich St. for 0.5 mi. to intersection with Rte. 7.

3.7   Go left on Rte. 7 for 0.6 mi. back to Red Lion Inn.

4.3   Total mileage.

Chesterwood extension.

1.7   Cross tracks and continue 0.1 mi. to intersection with Rte. 183.

1.8   Go right on Rte. 183 for 0.2 mi.

2.0   Go left on Mohawk Lake Rd. for 0.1 mi.

2.1   Go left, following Chesterwood directional sign for 0.5 mi.

2.6   Chesterwood

2.6   Continue ride. Bear right at 0.2 mi. and head downhill.

3.2   Go left at T intersection.

3.7   Go left on Rte. 183 for 1.1 mi. back to Glendale.

4.8   At Glendale, cross tracks and pick up shorter version at 1.7 mi. mark.

6.5   Total mileage of Chesterwood extension.

Variation for ride past the Norman Rockwell Museum and Berkshire Botanical Garden.

2.0   Rte. 183 at Mohawk Lake Rd. turn to Chesterwood as in Chesterwood extension. Continue N. on Rte. 183 for 0.3 mi. to the Norman Rockwell Museum on right; continue for another 0.6 mi. to Rte. 183's intersection with Rte. 102

2.9   Go right on Rte. 102 for 1.5 mi. to T intersection with clock tower, Congregational Church and Town Hall.

4.4   Go left for 0.4 mi. to Red Lion Inn.

4.8   Total mileage for second extension.

RIDE 8:

STOCKBRIDGE –
CHERRY HILL CHALLENGE

4.3 MILES / SHORT LOOP
6.5 MILES / LONGER LOOP
4.8 MILES / VARIATION

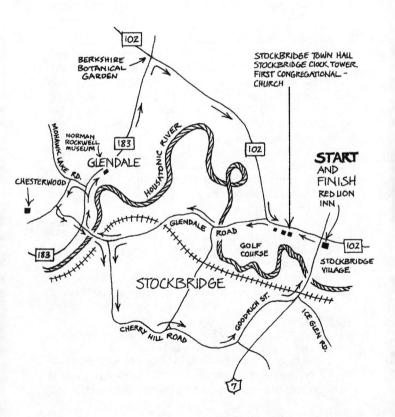

Ride 9: *Stockbridge – Housatonic Loop,* and **Ride 10:** *Stockbridge – Lenox Loop*

These two can be ridden separately or together. If ridden together, the total mileage is 24.8. One suggestion is to make them a morning and afternoon ride, with lunch at the Red Lion Inn.

Ride 9: *Stockbridge – Housatonic Loop*
10.6 miles if linked with Ride 10; 12.5 miles if loop is completed.

Start at the Red Lion Inn and head S. on Rte. 7, a main road with good shoulders, for 3 mi., a stretch that provides awesome views of the Monument Mtn. cliffs, just off the right handlebar.

At the 3-mi. mark, after a gradual uphill, there's a picnic area at the base of Monument Mtn. that is maintained, along with the trail system, by the Trustees of Reservations. An option here is to lock the bikes and take the fairly easy hike to the top of those cliffs, an elevation of 1,649 feet that provides a four-way view of the Berkshires. It was here, legend has it, that an Indian maiden, disappointed in love, leapt to her death. The ascent takes between three-quarters of an hour and an hour, and there are two choices of trails, both explained on a sign at the picnic area.

Whether or not the hike is chosen, continue the ride toward Gt. Barrington. In about 0.5 mi. it will head downhill, and in another 0.5 mi. leave the road at the sign pointing to Rte. 183, a right turn.

Continue downhill for 0.4 mi. and then go right on Rte. 183, pedaling 1.2 mi. to the Rising Paper Mill on the left with its expansive "mill pond," the dammed-up Housatonic, just beyond. The Rising mill is a splendid example of 19th-century mill architecture. As previously noted, when built in 1876, it was the largest paper mill in the world.

There's a good opportunity to stock up on fruit, meats and other goodies along this stretch. The Taft Farms stand, one of the larger ones in the county, is at the corner of Division St. and

Rte. 183, on the left, about 0.25 mi. after the right onto 183. And just before the village of Housatonic, but after passing the Rising Mill, stop at the Berkshire Mountain Bakery for an unusually tasty sourdough bread. The bakery also offers a bonus: a water bottle fill-up from water that has gone through the "super filtration" process used for making bread.

From the Rising Mill, follow Rte. 183 for another 1.1 mi. to Housatonic, taking a right after the bridge over the Housatonic River to start climbing gradually. The first impressive view, almost immediately on the right, is the remains of the once gigantic and still huge Monument Mt. Mill. Once abandoned, the mill now houses a few small enterprises.

The second view, in marked contrast to the aging mill, is the ever-young Housatonic River, with its lively rapids, that goes along the road on the right for about two miles. Farther up the road on the right, the ride passes a small hydroelectric plant that once supplied power to the Monument Mt. Mill.

Continue to Glendale, a village settled in 1760. The turnoff to Chesterwood, the summer house of the sculptor Daniel Chester French, is 3.3 mi. north of Housatonic. Go left on Mohawk Lake Rd. for 0.1 mi., then left for about 0.5 mi. to Chesterwood's entrance. About a mi. beyond the Chesterwood turnoff, Rte. 183 intersects with Rte. 102. The final section of this stretch, between Chesterwood and Rte. 102, passes the Norman Rockwell Museum on the right, .03 mi. beyond Mohawk Lake Rd. The Berkshire Botanical Garden is located at the intersection of Rtes. 183 and 102.

From the intersection the trip can return to the Red Lion Inn. Go right, follow Rte. 102 SE 1.5 mi. to the Stockbridge clock tower/Stockbridge Town Hall/First Congregational Church cluster of buildings. At this point turn left on Rte. 102 at the T intersection and ride 0.4 mi. back to the Red Lion Inn.

Summary: Ride 9

0.0   Start at Red Lion Inn and go south 4.0 mi. on Rte. 7.
       (Picnic spot at base of cliffs is at 3-mi. mark.) On
       downhill after rest area, spot sign pointing to Rte. 183.

4.0   Go right at sign for 0.4 mi..

4.4   Go right on Rte. 183, following it 6.2 mi. to intersection

with Rte. 102.
10.6   Continue straight for Ride 10. Or, go right on Rte. 102 for
       1.9 mi. back to Red Lion Inn.
12.5   Total mileage.

Ride 10: *Stockbridge – Lenox Loop*
*16.1 miles if started from Stockbridge; 14.2 miles if continued
from Ride 9.*

The ride starts at the Red Lion Inn and heads W. on Rte.
102 past the Stockbridge Town Hall, clock tower and the First
Congregational Church. Head N. on Rte. 102 for 1.5 mi. to the
Rte. 183 intersection, the end of Ride 9.

Go right (or straight if being continued from Ride 9), and
follow Rte. 183 toward Lenox, going underneath the Massachusetts Turnpike overpass and through the picturesque
hamlet of Interlaken.   Approximately 2.5 mi. from the
intersection of Rtes. 102 and 183, after a gradual uphill climb,
the rider will begin to catch glimpses of the Stockbridge Bowl.
There is public access to the bowl through an ample parking
lot at 3.1 mi. from the Rtes. 102 and 183 intersection, a fine
place for a picnic and for small boat watching on a summer
day. An alternative picnic site is Gould Meadows, on the
corner of Hawthorne St. nearly 1 mi. up from the boat-
launching area. The meadow, owned by the town of Stockbridge, offers one of the more spectacular views in the area.

The imposing redbrick building on the hill to the left
overlooking the Bowl in this stretch of the route is the former
Shadowbrook Jesuit monastery. For the past few years it has
been the home of Kripalu, a yoga retreat and holistic healing
center.

From the boat access the ride continues north on Rte. 183
and reaches the main gate of Tanglewood on the right in
another 1.1 mi. A bit of gradual climbing after Tanglewood
brings the trip to Lenox at the intersection of Rtes. 7A and 183,
practically at the doorstep of Town Hall, the brick building to
the right. If time permits, go straight, then left on Church St.
for food and shopping at a selection of boutiques.

From the Town Hall, follow Walker St., past three lovely old inns (Walker House on the right and the Candlelight and the Gateways on the left), then go right on Kemble St., passing Trinity Church on the corner at the left. On the right is the Kemble Inn, another classic.

Follow Kemble St. for about 0.5 mi. The National Music Center, which promises to be a major Berkshire attraction complete with a world-class music museum is on the right; the Canyon Ranch spa and resort, opened in 1989, is just beyond on the left, a $40 million restoration of the former Bellefontaine estate.

Kemble St. is also Rte. 7A and joins Rte. 7 about 0.5 mi. beyond Canyon Ranch. For a variation on the ride, cross Rte. 7 to Plunkett St. and almost immediately on the right is the entrance to The Mount, maintained by Edith Wharton Restoration, and the home of Shakespeare & Co.

Continuing the ride, follow Rte. 7 S., a downhill on wide road shoulders, passing the Foxhollow development on the left opposite Stockbridge Rd. (sometimes called Old Stockbridge Rd.). Start looking for landmarks such as the "Entering Lee" sign, then the High Lawn Farm sign on the left at Summer St. Look especially for West Rd. on the left, 0.5 mi. beyond the Highlawn Farm sign, and then take that left.

Follow West Rd. for 0.9 mi. until the first stop sign, at its intersection with Devon Rd. Go straight and ride for another 0.8 mi. to the second stop sign, this time at West and Stockbridge Rds. Go straight through. West becomes Church St., a relatively steep downhill for 1 mi. to the road's intersection with Rte. 102. Go right on Rte. 102 for an easy 2-mi. ride back to the Red Lion Inn.

Summary: Ride 10

(Either start at Red Lion Inn following Rte. 102 west for 1.9 mi. to intersection with Rte. 183 or continue from Ride 9. The 0.0 is where Rtes. 183 and 102 intersect.)

0.0 Intersection, Rtes. 183 and 102. Follow 183 north for 3.1 mi. and public access to Stockbridge Bowl on right.

3.1 At Stockbridge Bowl stop for picnic or keep going

straight 1.1 mi. to Tanglewood main gate and another 1.5 mi. to Lenox Center and Town Hall.

5.7   At Town Hall, follow Walker St. 0.2 mi. to Kemble St. (Rte.7A) on right.

5.9   Go right on Kemble St. for 1.3 mi. to intersection with Rte. 7 (The Mount and Edith Wharton Restoration, home of Shakespeare & Co., is reached by crossing Rte. 7 to Plunkett Street. Entrance is a few hundred yards along, on right.)

7.2   Go south on Rte. 7 for 1.0 mi., looking for sign for High Lawn Farm on left, then another 0.6 mi. to oblique left going off Rte. 7, West Rd.

8.8   Follow West Rd. (the oblique left) for 0.9 mi. to first stop sign. Go straight for 0.8 mi. to second stop sign. Go straight on Church St. for 1.0 mi. to intersection with Rte. 102.

11.5   Go right on Rte. 102, 2.0 mi. for return to Red Lion Inn.

13.5   Total mileage Ride 10.

Total mileage Rides 9 and 10: 24.1.

RIDE 10:

STOCKBRIDGE-LENOX LOOP

13.5 MILES

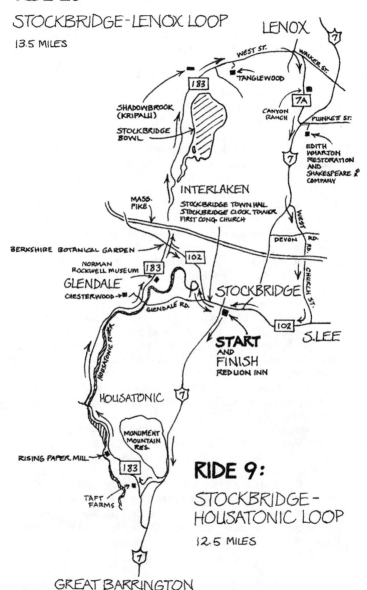

LENOX

WEST ST.

WALKER ST.

TANGLEWOOD

7A

CANYON RANCH

PLUNKETT ST.

SHADOWBROOK (KRIPALU)

STOCKBRIDGE BOWL

EDITH WHARTON RESTORATION AND SHAKESPEARE & COMPANY

INTERLAKEN

MASS. PIKE

STOCKBRIDGE TOWN HALL
STOCKBRIDGE CLOCK TOWER
FIRST CONG. CHURCH

WEST

DEVON RD.

BERKSHIRE BOTANICAL GARDEN

NORMAN ROCKWELL MUSEUM

183

102

CHURCH ST.

GLENDALE

CHESTERWOOD

STOCKBRIDGE

GLENDALE RD.

102

S. LEE

START
AND
FINISH
RED LION INN

HOUSATONIC RIVER

HOUSATONIC

7

MONUMENT MOUNTAIN RES.

RISING PAPER MILL

183

RIDE 9:

STOCKBRIDGE-HOUSATONIC LOOP

12.5 MILES

TAFT FARMS

7

GREAT BARRINGTON

Ride 11: *Stockbridge Bowl Ride-Around*
11.3 miles

This ride is not only pretty, it takes the visitor by most of the major attractions in the Stockbridge–Lenox area, including estates, Mission House, the Berkshire Botanical Garden, Tanglewood, the Stockbridge Bowl itself and Naumkeag.

The ride starts at the Red Lion Inn and heads west on Rte. 102 for 0.4 mi. and the scenic cluster of buildings that includes the Stockbridge Town Hall, the Stockbridge clock tower and the First Congregational Church. Turn right, following Rte. 102 for 1.5 mi. to its intersection with Rte. 183, where the ride again turns right.

Rte. 183 goes under the Mass. Pike and through the hamlet of Interlaken, climbing gradually to the Stockbridge Bowl and a public access way 3.1 mi. from the intersection of Rtes. 102 and 183. This is a good place for a picnic, but before deciding, consider what lies another 0.5 mi. ahead.

From the access continue on Rte. 183 for another 0.8 mi. and make a right at Hawthorne St., the south border of the Tanglewood grounds and the second good spot for a picnic because the view overlooks the Bowl with Monument Mtn. in the background. Named Gould Meadows, it is one of the more famous panoramas in the Berkshires. If it's a Sunday afternoon in July or August, the Boston Symphony Orchestra will be playing, adding to the charm of the surroundings. One word of warning, though. Traffic around Tanglewood on a Sunday afternoon when the BSO is playing is apt to be heavy. Parts of Gould Meadows may also be used for Tanglewood parking.

Continue the ride on Hawthorne St. At 0.7 mi. from Rte. 183 Hawthorne St. goes left to Lenox. Go straight, down a 0.5-mi. hill, past a Stockbridge Bowl cove on the right, then the Stockbridge Town Beach (open to residents and guests only), also on the right. Beyond the beach is the final 2-mi. descent of Prospect Hill. Bear right near the bottom, and the ride comes out directly opposite the Red Lion Inn.

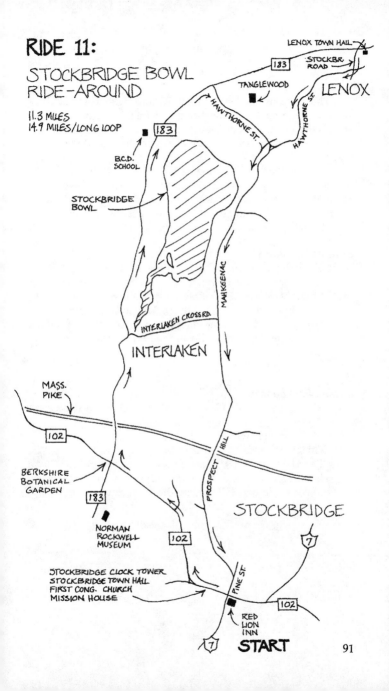

RIDE 11:

STOCKBRIDGE BOWL RIDE-AROUND

11.3 MILES
14.9 MILES/LONG LOOP

LENOX TOWN HALL
183
STOCKBR. ROAD
TANGLEWOOD
LENOX
HAWTHORNE ST.
HAWTHORNE ST.
183
B.C.D. SCHOOL
STOCKBRIDGE BOWL
MAHKEENAC
INTERLAKEN CROSS RD.
INTERLAKEN
MASS. PIKE
102
PROSPECT HILL
BERKSHIRE BOTANICAL GARDEN
183
STOCKBRIDGE
NORMAN ROCKWELL MUSEUM
102
7
STOCKBRIDGE CLOCK TOWER
STOCKBRIDGE TOWN HALL
FIRST CONG. CHURCH
MISSION HOUSE
PINE ST.
102
RED LION INN
7
START

The ride can also begin in Lenox, starting at Town Hall and then heading down Stockbridge Rd. for 0.3 mi., then right at Hawthorne St. and down a 1.5-mi. hill to the stop sign. Go left for 4.8 mi. to Stockbridge, picking up the ride at the 0.0 mark.

To avoid the final hill going back to Lenox, stay on Rte. 183 instead of going right on Hawthorne St. just before Tanglewood. From Hawthorne St. to Lenox Center on Rte. 183 is 1.7 mi. There's still a hill at the end but not so steep as the one on Hawthorne St. section.

Summary: Ride 11

0.0 From Red Lion Inn, head W. on Rte. 102 for 0.4 mi., then follow it right for 1.5 mi. to intersection with Rte. 183.

1.9 Go right on Rte. 183, following it 3.1 mi. to access to Stockbridge Bowl and another 0.8 mi. to Hawthorne St.

5.8 Go right on Hawthorne St., following it for 0.7 mi. until it turns left for Lenox. Go straight for another 4.8 mi. back to Stockbridge.

11.3 Total mileage.

If taken from Lenox:

0.0 Start at Town Hall. Go downhill on Stockbridge Rd. for 0.3 mi.

0.3 Go right on Hawthorne St.

1.8 Go left at T intersection with Mahkeenac Rd.

6.6 Red Lion Inn and 0.0 start for Ride 11. To return to Lenox, pick up Ride 11 at 5.8 mark, Hawthorne St.; then, making left turn, follow Hawthorne back to Lenox.

Ride 12: *The Five Village Workout:*
Stockbridge – Lenox – South Lee –Tyringham – Monterey
34.3 miles

This ride is ideal for bicyclists who enjoy a good day's workout over mostly rolling roads with varied scenery and no really formidable mountains. The ride starts at the Red Lion Inn, passes the Stockbridge Bowl, goes through Lenox, then heads south through mostly open agricultural country to Tyringham. After Tyringham it goes through a wooded area to Monterey, emerging in open country again on the way back to Stockbridge. A swim can be included either at Beartown State Forest, reached by a short side trip after going through Monterey, or at Lake Garfield.

From the Red Lion Inn the ride goes up Pine St., directly across from the inn, and bears left for a 2-mi. uphill over Prospect Hill, a way lined with estates on both sides and then the Stockbridge Bowl on the left. At the 4.6 mi. mark, after a second climb, the trip goes right on Hawthorne St., dips a little, then continues uphill 1.2 mi. to a stop sign and T intersection at Old Stockbridge Rd. Turn left for another climb of 0.3 mi. to the monument on top of the hill. Town Hall, a redbrick building, is on the right.

Since stores are few and far between on this trip, Lenox should be considered for purchases of take-out food. Try Church St., across and down Walker St. from Town Hall, for starters. The street and its surroundings are full of temptation for eating, drinking and shopping.

The ride then follows Rte. 7A (Walker St.) E. from Town Hall, picking up Kemble St. for a right turn 0.2 mi. beyond Town Hall. Go right on Kemble St., heading S. downhill past the National Music Center on the right and Canyon Ranch spa resort (the former Bellefontaine estate) on the left. Kemble St. (Rte. 7A) joins Rte. 7 in 1.3 mi.

As an option, cross Rte. 7 to Plunkett St. and almost immediately on the right is the entrance to the Mount, maintained by Edith Wharton Restoration and the home of Shakespeare & Co.

The ride, however, continues. Leaving Kemble St., go right on Rte. 7 for 1.6 mi., passing the Foxhollow development on the left and Stockbridge Rd. (also known as Old Stockbridge Rd.) directly across from Foxhollow on the right. Look for the High Lawn Farm sign on the left at Summer St. 1 mi. after Kemble St., then continue for another 0.6 mi. to West Rd., which comes in obliquely from the left. Follow the road through two stop signs, the first at 0.9 mi. from Rte. 7 at an intersection with Devon Rd., and the second 0.8 mi. beyond the first at an intersection with Stockbridge Rd.

The ride crosses the intersection, where the road name changes to Church St., and heads downhill for 1 mi. to its intersection with Rte. 102 in South Lee. The route goes left on Rte. 102 for 0.1 mi., where a sign points to the right to the Oak 'n Spruce resort. The right is taken, and almost immediately the road crosses the Housatonic River, then bears left on Meadow St., which goes by Oak 'n Spruce on the left and right.

Unlike most Berkshire rides, this one goes straight across the floor of the Tyringham Valley, a distance of 2.1 mi. on a road named Meadow St. About 1 mi. into the valley, bear left where the road forks.

Meadow St. meets Tyringham Rd. where the ride heads right, southeast for 4.1 mi. of beautiful views out over the Monument Mtn.–Tyringham Valley on the right. Highlights are the Tyringham Fine Arts Gallery (sculpture, prints, ceramics and glass), about 2 mi. along, and a sculpture that is a cottage, or vice versa, depending on the point of view. The road continues through the village of Tyringham to Monterey Rd. on the right.

Take the right and head back across the floor of the valley, 3.8 mi. At about the halfway point the name Monterey Rd. changes to Tyringham Rd. It then goes through some woods and up a steep 1.5 mi. climb to the town beach at Lake Garfield, a possible choice for a picnic and swim. The Monterey General Store is about 0.5 mi. beyond the beach on Rte. 23.

A side trip possibility is to the Bidwell House at the end of the Art School Rd. (a right where Monterey Rd. becomes Tyringham Rd), approx 1 mi. uphill on an unpaved road. The house was built around 1750 as the home of the Rev. Adonijah Bidwell, the first minister of "Township No. 1," which included both Monterey and Tyringham. Situated on 190 acres, the house is surrounded by woods crisscrossed with hiking trails. The house itself contains period furniture lovingly assembled by a group dedicated to its restoration. It's open from Memorial Day to Columbus Day, Tuesday–Sunday, and there's an admission fee.

After reaching Rte. 23, turn right for a gradual downhill and rolling 5.4 mi. The ride passes the Beartown State Forest entrance on the right and Rte. 57 on the left and continues to the intersection of Monument Valley Rd. on the right and Lake Buel Rd. on the left.

Take a right for the 4.6-mi. gradual uphill ride on Monument Valley Rd., which affords some impressive views of the Monument Mtn. cliffs near the end.

Monument Valley intersects with Rte. 7, with the Monument Mtn. Regional High School on the right. Go right for a 2.7-mi. mostly downhill ride back to the Red Lion Inn.

Summary: Ride 12

0.0   From Red Lion Inn, go across Main St. to Pine St. and bear left up Prospect Hill, a 2-mi. climb. At 4.6 mi. watch for Hawthorne St. turnoff.

4.6   Go right at Hawthorne St. for 1.2 mi. to stop sign.

5.8   Go left at stop sign on Stockbridge Rd. for 0.3 mi.

6.1   Town Hall, a redbrick building, on right. Go right for 0.2 mi., then right on Kemble St. (Rte. 7A), 1.3 mi. to Rte. 7. (the Mount and Edith Wharton Restoration, home of Shakespeare & Co., is reached by crossing Rte. 7 to Plunkett St. Entrance is a few hundred yards along on right.)

7.2   Go right on Rte. 7 for 1.0 mi., spotting High Lawn Farm sign on left and then continuing for another 0.6 mi. to oblique left, going off Rte. 7 on West Rd.

8.8   Follow West Rd., the oblique left, for 0.9 mi. through first stop sign, then another 0.8 mi. through second stop sign where West St. becomes Church St. Follow Church for 1.0 mi. downhill to intersection with Rte. 102.

11.5   Go left on Rte. 102 for 0.1 mi. to sign pointing to Oak 'n Spruce.

11.6   Go right on road going to Oak 'n Spruce, bear left on Meadow St. and follow for 2.1 mi. to T intersection with Tyringham Rd. About 1 mi. into the valley the road forks. Bear left.

13.7   Go right on Tyringham Rd. for 1.8 mi. to Tyringham Galleries on left.

15.5   Continue for 2.3 mi. to intersection with Monterey Rd. on right.

17.8   Go right on Monterey Rd. for 3.8 mi. to Rte. 23. Lake Garfield is on left, just before Rte. 23 with town beach.

21.6   Go right on Rte. 23 for 5.4 mi. to intersection with Monument Valley Rd. on right, Lake Buel Rd. on left.

27.0   Go right on Monument Valley Rd. for 4.6 mi. to Rte. 7.

31.6   Go right on Rte. 7 for 2.7 mi. back to Red Lion Inn.

34.3   Total mileage.

THE FIVE VILLAGE WORKOUT:
STOCKBRIDGE-LENOX-S.LEE-TYRINGHAM-MONTEREY

34.3 MILES

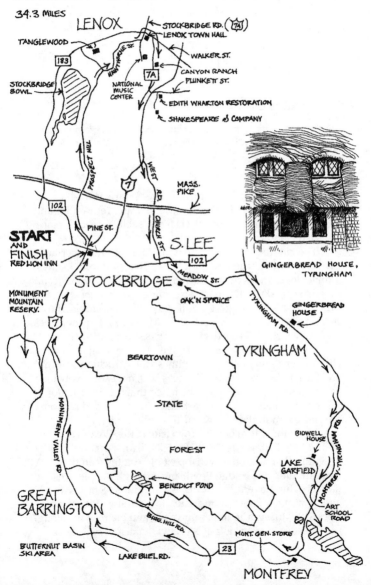

LENOX

TANGLEWOOD

STOCKBRIDGE RD. (7A)
LENOX TOWN HALL

WALKER ST.

183

CANYON RANCH
PLUNKETT ST.

HAWTHORNE ST.

7A

STOCKBRIDGE
BOWL

NATIONAL
MUSIC
CENTER

EDITH WHARTON RESTORATION

SHAKESPEARE & COMPANY

102

PROSPECT HILL

WEST RD.

I-7

MASS.
PIKE

CHURCH ST.

START
AND
FINISH
RED LION INN

PINE ST.

S. LEE

102

STOCKBRIDGE

MEADOW ST.

GINGERBREAD HOUSE,
TYRINGHAM

OAK'N SPRUCE

MONUMENT
MOUNTAIN
RESERV.

7

TYRINGHAM RD.

GINGERBREAD
HOUSE

BEARTOWN

TYRINGHAM

MONUMENT VALLEY RD.

STATE

FOREST

BIDWELL
HOUSE

GREAT
BARRINGTON

BENEDICT POND

BLUE HILL RD.

LAKE
GARFIELD

MONTEREY-TYRINGHAM RD.

ART
SCHOOL
ROAD

BUTTERNUT BASIN
SKI AREA

LAKE BUEL RD.

23

MONT. GEN. STORE

MONTEREY

CENTRAL COUNTY

Lenox: More Estates

Ride 13: *Lenox Landscaper*
30.9 miles; longer version, 34.2 miles

At one point or another the Lenox Landscaper encompasses most of the views, landscape, residential and industrial, that make the Berkshires such a special place. Hence the name.

The ride begins in Lenox with its aristocratic heritage, proceeds along the Stockbridge Bowl past old estates, Tanglewood and Kripalu (formerly the Shadowbrook Jesuit monastery), skirts the northern border of Stockbridge and proceeds south through the mill town of Housatonic. From there it continues south a bit over flat country, but then goes west and north through the farmscapes surrounding the town of Alford and on to W. Stockbridge. The final leg involves a climb over Lenox Mtn. (sometimes called Richmond Mtn.) and back to Lenox. Total mileage is 30.9, not excessively long as day rides go, but it should be noted that the final section is 2.2 mi. over Lenox Mtn., a part that can be avoided by going around the mountain for an additional 3.3 mi.

Begin the ride at Lenox Town Hall at Rte. 7A and the start of Rte. 183. Follow Rte. 183 S. for 5.7 mi. for a gradual rolling downhill that takes the cyclist past old estates, Tanglewood, Kripalu, the Stockbridge Bowl, and through the picturesque hamlet of Interlaken. The ride crosses the intersection with 102 and continues south along Rte. 183 passing the Norman Rockwell Museum at the 6.3-mi. mark, and then, .03 mi. along, the Chesterwood turnoff at Mohawk Lake Rd.

The ride follows the Housatonic River to the hulk of the Monument Mtn. mill in Housatonic and the town itself.

(Those interested in Victorian mill architecture might continue on Rte. 183 for 1.1 mi. to see the Rising Paper Company mill, an imposing four-story brick structure with two towers and a handsome mansard roof behind a row of tall spruces. The building is located at the end of a large mill pond created by a dam of the Housatonic.)

Rte. 183 passes the Monument Mt. mill, then comes to a stop sign at Pleasant St. Cross the intersection, leaving 183, and staying right of the railroad tracks. Proceed on Front St., which eventually becomes the Van Deusenville Rd. as the ride becomes flat. At 0.8 mi. on this leg it goes over the first railroad crossing, at 1.3 mi. it goes over a railroad crossing again, and at 1.8 mi. it comes to a T intersection with Division St. The private residence that used to be a church on the left was once the home of Alice Brock, who became famous as the proprietor of Alice's Restaurant, the title of the Arlo Guthrie song and film that was made in 1969. Guthrie has since bought the building and uses it as a center for charitable enterprises.

Go right at the intersection, cross Rte. 41 at 0.1 mi. and then ride straight at the first intersection for a total of 2 mi. to Division St.'s intersection with Alford Rd. Go right for a gradual uphill over rolling country for 1.6 mi. to Alford. On the approach to Alford's center, bear left at the Y, leaving the handsome New England church at the right. The ride is now on West Rd. Keep bearing right at a fork that comes up almost immediately.

Proceed gradually uphill for 5.2 mi. through luxuriously scenic countryside until West Rd.'s intersection with West Center Rd. Much of the land in this section is second-home property, owned by people from outside the county who have sought out quiet country places for retirement, vacations or investment.

Go left, then follow West Center Rd. for 3.3 mi. until its intersection with Rte. 102. At 102, go right for 1.2 mi. to Rte. 41 and W. Stockbridge, a village known for its boutiques, antiques, and opportunities for food. Go right on Rte. 41 for 0.3 mi. to the village's Main St.

The approach to the town is over a concrete bridge that spans the Williams River, with an antique place called the Shaker Mill on the right. Main St. is a sharp right after the bridge, Lenox Rd. is an uphill that's slightly to the left and Swamp Rd. is a third road, to the extreme left.

Take the middle road that's slightly diagonally left off the bridge and begin an immediate uphill. Riders will know they're on the correct road out of this somewhat confusing intersection, when they see an auto repair garage almost immediately on the left as the hill begins. There's also a sign at the intersection marking Lenox Rd. with directional arrows to Lenox and Tanglewood.

This is the beginning of a 2.1 mi. climb over Lenox Mtn., which ends at a T intersection near the top. Go right to head down the mountain for 1.7 mi. to the road's intersection with Rte. 183. Go left on Rte. 183, past Tanglewood's main entrance, for 1.6 mi. back to Town Hall in the center of Lenox.

Lenox Mtn. can be avoided by staying on Rte. 102, heading toward Stockbridge to its intersection with Rte. 183, a distance of 3 mi. Go left on Rte. 183 for the 5.7 mi. back to Lenox. Total mileage then would be 34.2 mi.

The ride can also start in Stockbridge at the Red Lion Inn by taking Rte. 102 W. for 1.9 mi. to its intersection with Rte. 183, where it turns left and heads toward Housatonic. Similarly, near the end at W. Stockbridge take Rte. 102 back to Stockbridge, a distance of 5 mi. The total mileage for the Stockbridge loop is 26.7.

Summary: Ride 13

0.0   From Lenox Town Hall, follow Rte. 183 S. for 5.7 mi. to intersection with Rte. 102.

5.7   Go straight through intersection, staying on Rte. 183 for 4.2 mi. (The Rockwell Museum is .06 mi. from the intersection. The turnoff to Chesterwood, studio of sculptor Daniel Chester French, is .03 mi. beyond the Rockwell Museum. Go right on Mohawk Lake Rd., then

RIDE 13:

LENOX LANDSCAPER

26.7 MILES / SHORT LOOP
30.9 MILES / MEDIUM LOOP
34.2 MILES / LONG LOOP

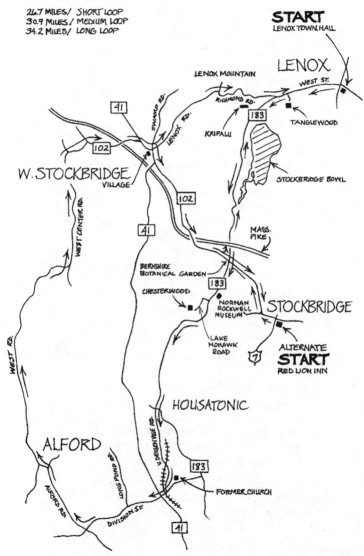

almost immediately left, following directional signs.)

9.9   Cross Pleasant St. in center of Housatonic to Front St.,
        which later becomes Van Deusenville Rd. First rail
        crossing is at .08 mi. from Housatonic center, second rail
        crossing at 1.3 mi. from Housatonic center. Follow this
        leg for total of 1.8 mi. to T.

11.7   Go right at T. Former church will be at left.

11.8   Cross Rte. 41 and continue on Division St. for 2.0 mi. and
        intersection with Alford Rd.

13.8   Go right for 1.6 mi. to Alford, go left at Y for West Rd.,
        passing church on right and bearing right at next fork,
        0.1 mi.

15.5   Follow West Rd. 5.2 mi. to intersection with West Center
        Rd.

20.7   Go left on West Center Rd. 3.3 mi. to intersection with
        Rte. 102.

24.0   Go right on Rte. 102 for 1.6 mi. to W. Stockbridge.

25.2   Go right on Rte. 41 for .03 mi.

25.5   Heading into W. Stockbridge, cross concrete bridge and
        go diagonally left across to Lenox Rd., which climbs
        Lenox Mtn. (Village Main St. is off to right.) Ride is on
        course if auto repair garage appears almost immedi-
        ately on left heading up Lenox Rd. Climb hill for 2.1 mi.

27.6   Go right at T and head down mountain for 1.7 mi. and
        intersection with Rte. 183.

29.3   Go left on Rte. 183 for 1.6 mi. back to Lenox Town Hall.

30.9   Total mileage.

If starting from Stockbridge:

0.0   From Red Lion Inn follow Rte. 102 W. for 1.9 mi. to
        intersection with Rte. 183, the 5.7 mi. marker for trip
        from Lenox. Go left. On return, at W. Stockbridge 25.5
        mi. marker, follow Rte. 102 back to Stockbridge for 5 mi.

26.7   Total mileage from Stockbridge.

If riders want to avoid Lenox Mtn. near the end:

From 25.5 at W. Stockbridge, head S. on Rte. 102 for 3 mi., go
left on Rte. 183 for 5.7 mi. back to Lenox.

Total mileage by avoiding Lenox Mtn.: 34.2.

Ride 14: *Lenox Meander*
5.9 miles; 7.3 miles with Pleasant Valley Sanctuary variation.

The ride goes around a hidden horseshoe-shaped valley, one of the few in The Berkshires, that begins at the Tanglewood main entrance and continues gradually uphill through idyllic scenery including a duck pond. A side trip can be made to the Pleasant Valley sanctuary, but it requires the stamina for a demanding hill.

The ride begins at Lenox Town Hall and goes down Stockbridge Rd. for 0.3 mi. and then goes right on Hawthorne St. for another 1.2 mi., all downhill, to a stop sign. Take the right and ride along a flat stretch, with the Stockbridge Bowl on the left and the high hedges of Tanglewood's south side on the right, for 0.7 mi. until the road intersects with Rte. 183. Just before Rte. 183 a Gould Meadows on the left, overlooking the Bowl makes a good picnic spot.

Go right on Rte. 183 for 0.3 mi.; then directly opposite Tanglewood's main entrance take a left on the 3.2-mi. Under Mountain Rd., which goes up a gradual hill, passing a lovely duck pond on the left before reaching the top of the hill.

Past the duck pond the road hugs the side of the valley. The mountain on the left is almost like a wall, giving the road its name. A look to the rear will reveal a beautiful pocket valley.

At the head of the valley the road goes right and leads back to Lenox, where it becomes Cliffwood St. and intersects with Main St. at an angle. Go right for 0.2 mi. to Town Hall, where the ride started.

The variation to the Pleasant Valley Sanctuary comes toward the end of Under Mountain Rd., before it becomes Cliffwood St. From Tanglewood's main gate follow Under Mountain Rd. for 2.2 mi. around the head of the valley. Take a sharp left on Reservoir Rd. and climb the hill for 1.3 mi. to the sanctuary's entrance. While the hill is not for sissies, it is also not impossible. The Lenox reservoir is on the right, about 0.5

mi. before the sanctuary entrance. Bear right at the road fork near the reservoir. At this point the road surface changes to dirt.

Summary: Ride 14

0.0   From Lenox Town Hall go down Stockbridge Rd. for 0.3 mi.

0.3   Go right on Hawthorne St. for 1.2 mi. to stop sign.

1.5   Go right at stop sign for 0.7 mi. Stockbridge Bowl is on left, Tanglewood on right.

2.2   Go right on Rte. 183 for 0.3 mi. and Tanglewood main entrance.

2.5   Go left on Under Mountain Rd., just opposite Tanglewood main entrance. Road goes up and down gradually and eventually becomes Cliffwood St. when it gets back to center of Lenox. Total distance is 3.2 mi.

5.7   At Main St., Lenox, go right for 0.2 mi. back to Town Hall.

5.9   Total mileage.

Pleasant Valley Sanctuary variation.

4.7   Go left on Reservoir Rd. from Under Mountain Rd. Climb for 1.3 mi. to sanctuary entrance. Return same way.

7.3   Total mileage with sanctuary variation.

RIDE 14:

LENOX MEANDER

5.9 MILES
7.3 MILES / VARIATION

PLEASANT VALLEY WILDLIFE SANTUARY

RESERVOIR

RESERVOIR RD.

UNDER MOUNTAIN RD.

CLIFFWOOD ST.

7A

183

LENOX

WEST ST.

RICHMOND RD.

HAWTHORNE ST.

TANGLEWOOD

HAWTHORNE ST.

STOCKBRIDGE RD.

WALKER ST.

183

START
LENOX TOWN HALL

THE SHED,
TANGLEWOOD

STOCKBRIDGE BOWL

Ride 15: *Lenox All-Aboard*
5.9 miles

The ride may well become popular during the next few years as a way to combine a day of bicycle and rail travel. As of late 1994, however, such a combination remains a dream.

The ride goes by the old Lenox train station in Lenoxdale that is being restored by the Berkshire Scenic Railway, an organization of volunteers that has acquired both locomotives and passenger cars. Although the rail group ran trips during the 1980s between Lee and Gt. Barrington, the future of such trips remains uncertain because of a murky situation regarding track ownership and liability. If the situation is ever resolved, Berkshire Scenic will sponsor rail excursions.

In any event, even if the trains aren't running, a visit to the station and the developing rail museum provides an interesting stop midway through the trip. The ride is also easily combined with boutique and food shopping in the center of Lenox.

The ride to the station follows the old Berkshire Street Railway trolley spur between the station and Lenox. Old-timers tell the story that the wealthy cottagers in Lenox didn't want the railroad to go through the town because they feared a resulting commercialism of the town's bucolic setting.

The ride begins on the corner of Church and Walker Sts., approximately opposite Lenox Town Hall. Head down Church St. to Housatonic St. and then go right to Rte. 7, 1 mi. from where the ride began.

Cross Rte. 7 and continue downhill, going through the East St. intersection, for a total of 1.2 mi. At the bottom of the hill, Crystal St. takes an abrupt right. Go left for a few hundred yards to the Berkshire Railway Museum.

To return to Lenox, follow Crystal St., a flat section, for 1.2 mi. to Lenoxdale and then go right on Walker St. (Mill St. comes in from left over a bridge.) Follow Walker for a gradual uphill climb of 1.5 mi. to Rte. 7, cross the highway, and continue for 1 mi. more back to where the ride began.

RIDE 15:
LENOX ALL-ABOARD
5.9 MILES

CURTIS HOTEL &
EGLESTON MONUMENT,
LENOX

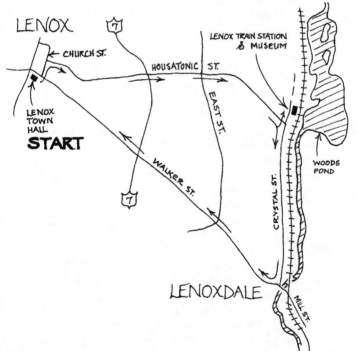

LENOX

CHURCH ST.

LENOX TRAIN STATION & MUSEUM

HOUSATONIC ST.

EAST ST.

LENOX TOWN HALL **START**

WALKER ST.

CRYSTAL ST.

WOODS POND

LENOXDALE

MILL ST.

Summary: Ride 15

0.0   Ride begins at corner of Church and Walker. Follow
       Church for 0.1 mi.
0.1   Go right on Church for 0.9 mi. to Rte. 7.
1.0   Cross Rte. 7 and continue for 1.2 mi. to bottom of hill
       where Crystal St. goes right to Lenoxdale. Go left for
       a few hundred yards to Lenox train station and
       Berkshire Scenic Railway.
2.2   Follow Crystal St. to Lenoxdale, 1.2 mi.
3.4   Go right on Walker St. for 1.5 mi. to Rte. 7.
4.9   Cross Rte. 7 for 1 mi. trip back to corner of Church
       and Walker.
5.9   Total mileage.

Ride 16: *Estates Odyssey*
5 miles

Although short, the ride gives some sense of the grand estates in the Lenox area that were built between 1890 and 1910 by more than three dozen millionaires of the period. The ride goes by the National Music Center; Canyon Ranch, a health spa located on the former Bellefontaine estate; and The Mount, where Edith Wharton, a prominent early-20th-century author, lived. Its route circles Cranwell, another one of the former estates and now a resort, conference and condominium center. Along Plunkett St. it provides a view of Foxhollow on Laurel Lake, a fourth grand estate that now boasts condominiums.

Bellefontaine was built in 1896 by millionaire Giraud Foster of New York City as a replica of the Petit Trianon at Versailles, France. Edith Wharton designed and built The Mount in 1902, reflecting themes she had already expressed as an author. Cranwell was originally owned by Henry Ward Beecher, a Boston preacher who bought the 250-acre farm in 1853. The property came into its own as an estate in 1892 when it was sold to John Sloane of New York City after he tired of the faster pace of summer society in Newport, RI. Foxhollow is located across Laurel Lake and can be seen at a distance from Plunkett St. The property was bought in 1887 by George Westinghouse, an electrical genius, inventor and industrial giant of the time, and developed over a period of years, mostly under the supervision of his wife, Margaret Erskine W. Westinghouse. The estate is now owned by Kripalu, a nearby spa.

The ride begins at Town Hall, next to the monument, and heads out Walker St., leaving Town Hall on the right and Church St. on the left. At 0.2 mi. it turns right on Kemble St., with Trinity Church on the left, and goes downhill, passing the National Music Center on the right, Canyon Ranch on the left. Rte. 7 and a traffic light is at the 1.5 mi. mark.

Cross Rte. 7 for Plunkett St.; the driveway to the Mount is almost immediately on the right. There, Edith Wharton Restoration sponsors a number of activities and events during the summer months, and Shakespeare & Co. performs outdoors on the grounds.

Continue on Plunkett St., catching glimpses of Foxhollow and Laurel Lake on the right, for 0.9 mi. to Rte. 20. Cross Rte. 20 to East St., one of the bordering streets of the Cranwell complex. Follow East St. for 0.7 mi. to Walker St. and then go left for another 0.9 mi. to Rte. 7. The Cranwell golf course is on the left. Cross Rte. 7 and continue on Walker St. for 1 mi. back to Lenox Town Hall.

Summary: Ride 16

0.0   Lenox Town Hall. Head out Walker St. in front of building.
0.2   Go right on Kemble St., leaving Trinity Church on left.
0.6   National Music Center on right.
0.9   Canyon Ranch spa on left.
1.5   Cross Rte. 7 at traffic light for Plunkett St. Driveway to the Mount is almost immediately on right as Plunkett St. begins. Follow Plunkett St. for 0.9 mi.
2.4   Cross Rte. 20 for East St. Cranwell resort is at left. Follow East St. for 0.7 mi.
3.1   Go left on Walker St. for 0.9 mi.
4.0   Cross Rte. 7 at traffic light and continue for 1 mi. back to Lenox Town Hall.
5.0   Total mileage.

RIDE 16:
ESTATES ODYSSEY
5 MILES

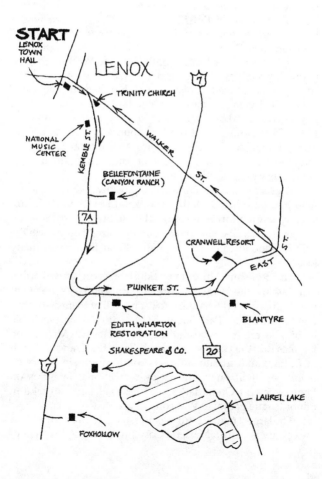

Pittsfield: Berkshire's Urban Place

Pittsfield, a city of 44,000 and the county's retail, financial and governmental center, has several interesting attractions that make it easy to spend a day or just a couple of hours. North St., the main shopping area, has stores, banks and restaurants as well as the Berkshire Hilton, the county's largest and most modern hotel. More shopping is available just to the north of Pittsfield in the Coltsville area where Rtes. 8 and 9 intersect and at the Berkshire Mall, located between Rtes. 7 and 8 in the town of Lanesborough. Park Square is the hub for North, South, East and West streets, the main thoroughfares that form the skeleton for the city's street layout. Ringed by historic and dignified buildings, it is the original village square and about all that remains of the city's agricultural heritage. In 1810, the year of its founding, Pittsfield was the site of the first county fair in the United States. Organized by the Berkshire Agricultural Society, its purpose was the improvement of knowledge about agriculture as well as for the selling of livestock.

The society and the fair were inspired by Elkanah Watson, who had introduced Merino sheep to the U.S. in Berkshire County in an effort to improve the quality of textiles being made in local mills. His county-fair idea caught on all over the country, and such events are still regular features in many locales.

The Berkshire Museum on South St. is certainly worth a visit, as are the Berkshire Athenaeum, the city's excellent public library, and Berkshire Artisans. All of them are only a few minutes from Park Square. Other attractions, reachable by bicycle, are Arrowhead, the home of Herman Melville on Holmes Rd.; the Hancock Shaker Village; the Crane Museum in Dalton; and, in late summer, South Mountain Concerts. Swimmers will enjoy the city's recreational facilities on Pontoosuc and Onota lakes, and baseball fans can take in minor league games at Wahconah Park.

The largest manufacturing industry in both Pittsfield and the county is Martin Marietta Corp., with an employment of nearly 2,000. Martin Marietta acquired the former GE Aerospace plant in 1993 through a merger, thus ending nearly a century of General Electric's dominance of the county's economy. GE had originally established itself in Pittsfield when it bought the technology and the factory of William Stanley of Gt. Barrington. Stanley had invented transformers as a way of handling alternating current. GE made transformers in Pittsfield until 1986, when it shut the operation down as demand for its projects ebbed.

However, another one of GE's major businesses, GE Plastics, maintains its world headquarters in Pittsfield, employing just over 600. Plastics' pioneering work resulted in dramatic business growth during the 1980s. As a result, the city is a center of international activity in the development of different kinds of polymers, or plastics.

Pittsfield is also home to a number of smaller industries, with many of them making plastics products.

In the areas of culture and education, Berkshire Community College on outer West St. and a number of other community-based organizations provide an increasingly rich cultural life. Groups include the Berkshire Ballet, the Berkshire Public Theatre, Berkshire Artisans, the Berkshire Museum, and South Mountain Concerts. In 1994 an effort had begun to establish an American Graphic Arts Museum in the downtown.

All of the Pittsfield rides begin at the information booth on the east side of Park Square next to the County Courthouse. The booth provides listings for events and suggestions for accommodations. More detailed information about Pittsfield may be obtained from the Central Berkshire Chamber of Commerce office on the ground floor of the Tierney Building on West St., across from the Berkshire Hilton. And more detailed information about the county is available at the Berkshire Visitor's Bureau, which occupies a ground floor office at the Berkshire Hilton.

The major attractions in Pittsfield and the rides that include them on their routes are:

Arrowhead, 780 Holmes Rd. (Rides 18, 20)

In 1850, Herman Melville moved his family from New York City to Pittsfield, seeking a quiet place to write. He purchased a farmhouse that he named Arrowhead and then wrote *Moby Dick*, his most famous work, in an upstairs study that overlooks the twin humps of Mt. Greylock, which slightly resemble a whale, the subject of *Moby Dick*. Arrowhead is owned and operated by the Berkshire County Historical Society, which has a rich collection of historical offerings about both Melville and the county. Open daily Memorial Day weekend through Labor Day, 10–5. Labor Day–Oct. 31, Fri., Sat., Sun., Mon. 10–5.

Berkshire Artisans, 28 Renne Ave.

No ride goes by the gallery operated by Berkshire Artisans, but it's only a few minutes away from Park Square. Take Allen St. off the square, go past City Hall, cross Fenn for Renne Ave., a short jog to the left. The center is down a few yards on the right. The group operates the city's community arts center, which has regularly scheduled art exhibits. Open year-round, Mon.–Fri., 11–5; Sat., 12–5.

Berkshire Athenaeum, 1 Wendell Ave.

The three-level brick and glass public library is located almost directly behind the tourist information booth across Wendell Ave. The library features a comfortable reading room, a Local Authors Room, a Local History Room and a Herman Melville Room. Open Mon.–Thurs., 9–9; Fri., 9–5; Sat., 10–5. (July & Aug.: Mon., Wed., Fri. 9–5, Tues. and Thurs., 9–9; Sat., 10–1.)

Berkshire Museum, South St.

The museum is only a couple of minutes away from Park Square, whether on bike or foot. Just head toward the Berkshire Hilton from the information booth, then turn left on South St.

Small enough to tour in about an hour, the museum has a Native American classroom and an aquarium in its basement. Other offerings include art by American and European masters, an ancient civilizations gallery, and an outstanding collection of exotic shells, gemstones and minerals. Open year-round, Tues.–Sat., 10–5; Sun., 1–5. Closed Mon. except July & Aug. Fee except 10–noon Wed. & Sat.

Canoe Meadows, Holmes Rd. (Rides 18, 19, 20)

The 262-acre property bordering the Housatonic River is owned and maintained by the Massachusetts Audubon Society as a companion operation to the Pleasant Valley Sanctuary in Lenox. The facility, for passive recreation, is completely natural except for a replica of an Indian wigwam, a wildlife observation area and boardwalks. Picnicking is allowed, but there are no tables, and trash must be packed out. Open year-round 7 a.m. to dusk. Fee.

Crane Museum, Rte. 9, Dalton. (Ride 19)

Crane & Co., Dalton, makes all the paper on which U.S. currency is printed and also manufactures other high quality rag content lines of paper. The one-room museum behind the company's headquarters off Rtes. 8 and 9 was originally a mill. Through models, photos and paper samples, the museum tells how fine paper is made. Open June to mid-Oct., Mon.–Fri., 2–5. Free

Hancock Shaker Village, junction of Rtes. 20 and 41. (Ride 17)

The village is one of 19 settlements established in the 18th and 19th centuries by the Shakers, a religious sect that believed that Christ had returned to Earth in the form of Mother Ann Lee, the sect's founder. Communal living, a spartan life, celibacy and the concept that work is a form of religious worship were all elements of their fundamental beliefs. In 1790 they established a village in Hancock that reached its peak between 1830 and 1840. By the time the last Shakers left the village in 1959, most of the buildings had deteriorated. By 1990 a non-profit group that had taken over the property had carefully restored 20 of the buildings, including a round stone barn, architecturally considered the most important building. The barn was designed to allow one man to feed an entire herd of cattle because each animal faced inward in a circle of stanchions. Other buildings have furniture and other arrangements that reflect the Shakers' constant effort to seek more efficient ways of doing things. The museum has working craftspeople in several exhibits, a historic working farm, herb and vegetable gardens and an extensive museum shop as well as a number of events during its season. Open April–Oct. Fee.

South Mountain Concerts, Rte. 7

Founded in 1918 in a summer home 1 mi. south of Pittsfield off Rte. 7, the performers offer chamber music concerts on Sunday afternoons in late summer and fall in a 500-seat hall with outstanding acoustics. Programs feature such internationally known groups as the Beaux Arts Trio, the New World String Quartet and the Tokyo String Quartet, who perform in programs designed to please serious music lovers.

Ride 17: *Pittsfield-Hancock Shaker Village-*
W. Stockbridge Loop
23.5 miles; shorter version, 18.3 miles

Riders can learn about the Shakers, who would have loved their form-follows-function two wheelers, then enjoy one of the county's longer and more gradual downhills, stop to savor the delights of W. Stockbridge and then take the slow boat home on a gradual but thoroughly enjoyable uphill to Pittsfield. And if it all sounds like it's too much, there's a bail-out loop that cuts the trip by nearly 5 mi.Begin at Park Square in Pittsfield, the small park surrounded by traffic that is the hub for the spokes of North, South, East and West Sts. Head S. on South St. (Rte. 7) for 0.2 mile to W. Housatonic St. (Rte. 20), where the ride goes right. The traffic is heavy at this point, but the ride improves after about 1 mi. when the road widens, and in another 1 mi. it begins to have shoulders. Follow Rte. 20 for 4.3 mi. to Rte. 41 coming in from the left. Just beyond is the entrance to the Hancock Shaker Village.

Follow Rte. 41 S. for 8.4 mi. through beautiful farm countryside, generally a downhill on good pavement with only a few gentle hills. Rte. 295, going right to New York State, comes in at 3.5 mi.; ride another 1.3 mi. and look for the Richmond General Store on the left.

At this point the ride can be shortened. Go over the rail-road bridge and take an immediate and sharp left on Lenox Rd.   Follow Lenox Rd. for 1.2 mi. to its intersection with Swamp Rd. Take a left and head back to W. Housatonic St., 6.5 mi. Go right on W. Housatonic St., the way the ride began, for 0.9 mi., then left on South St. back to Park Square, 0.2 mi.

The longer version stays straight on Rte. 41 for another 3.4 mi. to W. Stockbridge. With its assortment of shops the village invites exploration or at least a stop for some quick food.

To head back to Pittsfield make a sharp, almost hairpin left turn as Rte. 41 enters the village, and head N. on Swamp Rd., a 9.5 mi. stretch. In about 1 mi., where Cone Hill Rd. comes in at an oblique left, bear right to stay on course. Swamp Rd.

goes gradually uphill, again through some beautiful farmscapes, with Lenox Mtn. off to the right, then a nice passage through woods. At the Pittsfield line it becomes Barker Rd. and then ends at W. Housatonic St. (Rte. 20), the first leg of the ride's beginning. Bartlett's Orchards, about halfway along on the right, operates a popular outlet for apples and cider when both are in season. There's also a Friendly Ice Cream establishment on the corner of W. Housatonic St. and Barker Rd.

At W. Housatonic St., go right for 1.1 mi. to South St., then left for 0.2 mi. back to Park Square.

Summary: Ride 17

0.0   Park Square. Go S. on South St. (Rte. 7) for 0.2 mi.
0.2   Go right on W. Housatonic St. (Rte. 20) for 4.3 miles, where Rte. 41 comes in from left. Just beyond is Hancock Shaker Village.
4.5   Follow Rte. 41 S. for 8.4 mi. to W. Stockbridge.

Ride can be shortened by taking a left on Lenox Rd. at 9.5 mi., just after Richmond General Store, following it for 1.2 mi., then going left again on Swamp Rd. for 6.5 mi. to W. Housatonic St. Go right on W. Housatonic St. for 0.9 mi., then left on South St. for 0.2 mi. back to Park Square. Total mileage for short version is 18.3.

12.9   Take sharp, almost hairpin left and head N. on Swamp Rd., which becomes Barker Rd. at Pittsfield line, for 9.5 mi.
22.4   Go right on W. Housatonic for 0.9 mi.
23.3   Go left on South St. for 0.2 mi. to Park Square.
23.5   Total mileage.

RIDE 17:

PITTSFIELD-HANCOCK SHAKER VILLAGE-
WEST STOCKBRIDGE LOOP

18.3 MILES / SHORT LOOP
23.5 MILES / LONG LOOP

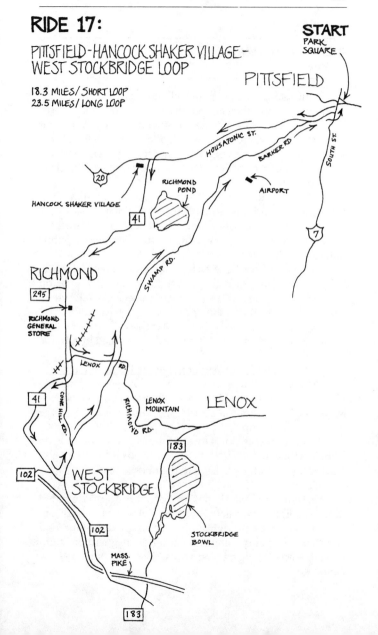

Ride 18: *Moby Dick*
11.2 miles

With apologies to Herman Melville, this meander around the southeast of Pittsfield and into a corner of Lenox mixes attractive countryside, Pittsfield residential streets and a visit to Arrowhead, where Herman Melville wrote *Moby Dick* in a second-floor study. A window in that study provides a spectacular view of the whalelike twin-hump profile of Mt. Greylock, 20 mi. to the north.

As do all of the Pittsfield rides, this one begins at the Park Square information booth. Walk the bikes along the sidewalk in front of the County Courthouse to Wendell Ave., the corner across from the Berkshire Athenaeum, Pittsfield's public library.

Ride down Wendell Ave. for a block, then take a left at the light on E. Housatonic St. Go right at the next light on Appleton Ave., go about a block to a triangle intersection, then left over a bridge, then a short right, staying on Appleton Ave. In about 0.2 mi. take a left on Williams St., and then ride for 0.5 mi. to its intersection with Holmes Rd., controlled by a traffic light.

Consider the option of going right for 0.3 mi. for a visit to Canoe Meadows, a place for a sit-down picnic along the Housatonic River. The Meadows, which is maintained by the Massachusetts Audubon Society, may also be visited on the return leg of the trip.

To continue the ride, cross Holmes Rd. and continue on Williams for another 0.5 mi. to E. New Lenox Rd. on the right, marked by a small white sign in the middle of a landscaped triangle.

Go right on E. New Lenox for a delightful 3-mi. downhill through a lightly populated section. October Mtn. begins to loom on the left; on the right as the ride progresses is farmland and then, quite surprisingly, a cluster of spaghettilike high-voltage electric transmission wires. The ride ends at New Lenox Rd.

The left goes to October Mtn. The ride, however, goes right for 1.1 mi., first crossing the Housatonic River, until it intersects with East St. Go right at the intersection for 0.9 mi. and Holmes Rd.

Go right on Holmes Rd. and head toward Pittsfield. Arrowhead will be on the left, 0.5 mi. along. It's a place to become steeped in Melville and Berkshire history and, if the day is clear, share Melville's inspiring view of Mt. Greylock.

Continue the ride back to Pittsfield for another 1.5 mi. to the intersection with Williams St. marked by the traffic light, the same as on the trip's first leg. Canoe Meadows is on the right, just before the intersection. Go left on Williams for 0.5 mi., go right on Appleton Ave., then left over the bridge, up a hill to a traffic light, then left again. The ride follows E. Housatonic St. for three blocks to the light at Wendell Ave. Take a right for a block to the start-finish at the Park Square information booth.

Summary: Ride 18

0.0   Park Square information booth.
0.1   Go right on Wendell Ave.
0.3   Go left at traffic light on E. Housatonic St.
0.5   Go right at traffic light on Appleton Ave.
0.8   After short downhill, bear left at intersection, cross bridge over Housatonic River, go right on Appleton Ave.
1.1   Go left on Williams St.
1.6   Cross Holmes Rd. at traffic light and keep going straight on Williams St. Or go right on Holmes Rd. for 0.3 mi. to Canoe Meadows on left.
2.1   Go right on E. New Lenox Rd.
5.1   Go right on New Lenox Rd.
6.2   Go right on East Rd.
7.1   Go right on Holmes Rd.
7.6   Arrowhead on left.
9.6   Go left on Williams St. at traffic light.

10.1 Go right on Appleton Ave., then left over bridge and right again.

10.7 Go left on E. Housatonic St. at traffic light marking intersection with Appleton.

11.0 Go right on Wendell Ave. at traffic light.

11.2 Wendell Ave. intersects with East St. Go left for information booth.

11.2 Total mileage.

RIDE 18:

MOBY DICK

11.2 MILES

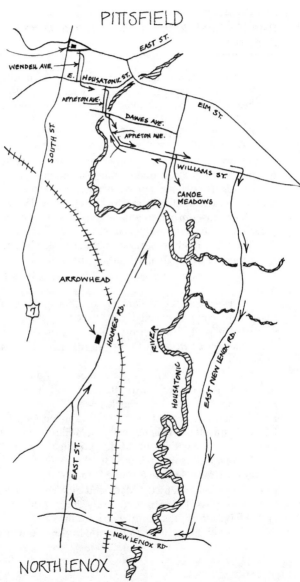

PITTSFIELD

EAST ST.

WENDELL AVE.

E. HOUSATONIC ST.

APPLETON AVE.

DAWES AVE.

APPLETON AVE.

ELM ST.

WILLIAMS ST.

CANOE MEADOWS

SOUTH ST.

ARROWHEAD

HOLMES RD.

HOUSATONIC RIVER

EAST NEW LENOX RD.

7

EAST ST.

NEW LENOX RD.

NORTH LENOX

Ride 19: *Pittsfield-Dalton-Hinsdale and Back*
22.6 miles

This ride is recommended for anyone with an interest in money. If you have U.S. currency in your pocket, the paper that bears the printing was made at Crane & Co. and you will ride right past its plant.

One of the older papermakers in the United States, Crane was established in 1801 and has been under continuous ownership by the Crane family from that date. While the company makes a full line of fine papers, it is particularly known for its currency and security papers. Since 1879 the company has made all the paper for U.S. currency. The company operates a museum of papermaking next to its office building in Dalton, where admission is free.

The ride is relatively easy until the last leg, where it leaves Rte. 8, then climbs for about 1.5 mi. into the Pittsfield watershed. From there it's downhill and flat, all the way back to Park Square.

The ride begins at the Park Square information booth. To make sure you're headed right, walk the bikes along the sidewalk in front of the County Courthouse to Wendell Ave., the corner across from the Berkshire Athenaeum, Pittsfield's public library.

Ride down Wendell Ave. for a block, then take a left at the light on E. Housatonic St. Go right at the next light on Appleton Ave., go about a block to a triangle intersection, then left over a bridge, then a short right, staying on Appleton Ave. In about 0.2 mi. take a left on Williams St. Follow Williams St. for 0.5 mi. to its intersection with Holmes Rd., controlled by a traffic light.

If a picnic or rest stop is in order this early on, go right on Holmes Rd. for 0.3 mi. to Canoe Meadows, a passive recreation area maintained by the Massachusetts Audubon Society. Otherwise cross Holmes and continue along Williams St. to its end at Division St., the 3.5 mi. mark for the ride.

Go left on Division St., a flat ride for 1.6 mi., then take a right at the traffic light, on South St., heading toward Dalton. (The left is East St., which would take the ride back to Pittsfield. If a bailout is considered here, be aware that traffic on East St. in Pittsfield is heavy.)

South St. is a curvy but manageable 1.6 mi. uphill to Rte. 9 in Dalton. Crane & Co. is just to the right at the intersection, and the museum is just beyond the headquarters building.

From Crane & Co., go right on Rte. 9, then, within a matter of yards, right again on Housatonic St. for an easy 2.1 mi. to Rte. 8, heading S. to Hinsdale and Becket. Follow Rte. 8, climbing uphill in steps to Hinsdale, where Rte. 143 comes in from the left.

If you like to photograph handsome New England churches, take a left on 143 and the First Congregational Church is almost immediately on the left.

The ride continues on Rte. 8 south. In 1 mi. a bridge crosses the Housatonic, followed by a second bridge crossing the railroad. Keep going for another 2 mi. and then at the crest of the hill look for a road merging in from the right at a sharp angle, creating a hairpin turn. The road is unmarked but called either the Blotz Rd. or the Pittsfield Rd. Begin a 1.5-mi. climb, with a few flat stretches for relief, into the Pittsfield watershed area.

From the top it's downhill all the way to Williams St. on a road bordered on each side by woods. Pittsfield's Sackett Reservoir will be on the left, going down, about 0.75 mi. from the summit. The name of the road on the descending portion into Pittsfield is Kirchner.

Kirchner goes into Williams, the first leg of the trip. As before, ride 1.6 mi. on Williams St. to the traffic light, cross Holmes Rd. (or go left for a side trip to Canoe Meadows), continue on Williams until Appleton, go right, then left over the bridge and right again, up a small hill to the traffic light at E. Housatonic.

Go left for 3 blocks, then right on Wendell Ave. to East St. Look left for the sidewalk to the information booth.

Summary: Ride 19

0.0   Park Square information booth.
0.1   Go right on Wendell Ave.
0.3   Go left at traffic light on E. Housatonic St.
0.5   Go right at traffic light on Appleton Ave.
0.8   After short downhill, bear left at intersection, cross bridge over Housatonic River, go right on Appleton Ave.
1.1   Go left on Williams St.
1.6   Williams crosses Holmes Rd. at traffic light. (Or go right on Holmes for .3 mi. to Canoe Meadows on left.)
3.5   Go left on Division St. Williams St. ends.
5.1   Go right on South St. at traffic light. (East St. goes left back to Pittsfield.)
6.7   Crane & Co. Museum of Papermaking.
6.7   Go right on Rte. 8 but then take an almost immediate right again on Housatonic St.
8.9   Go right on Rte. 8 heading S. toward Hinsdale.
11.2 Rte. 143 comes in at left.
12.2 Bridge crosses Housatonic, followed by second bridge over railroad tracks.
14.4 Go right at crest of hill, making hairpin turn on road to Pittsfield.
16.8 Sackett Reservoir on left.
19.1 Williams St. and Division St. Go straight on Williams.
21.0 Williams crosses Holmes Rd. Traffic light. Go straight.
21.5 Go right on Appleton Ave., then left over bridge and right again.
22.1 Go left on E. Housatonic St. at traffic light marking intersection with Appleton.
22.4 Go right on Wendell Ave. at traffic light.
22.6 Wendell Ave. intersects with East St. Go left for information booth.
22.6 Total mileage.

143

First Congregational Church

8

HINSDALE

8

HOUSATONIC RIVER

8

DALTON

HOUSATONIC ST.

8A

9

CRANE MUSEUM

SOUTH ST.

DIVISION ST.

KIRCHNER RD.

BLOTZ RD.

SACKETT RESERVOIR

PITTSFIELD

EAST ST.

E. HOUSATONIC ST.

WILLIAMS ST.

CANOE MEADOWS

HOLMES RD.

APPLETON AVE.

NORTH ST.

START
PARK SQUARE
INFO BOOTH

WENDELL AVE.

SOUTH ST.

RIDE 19:
PITTSFIELD-DALTON-HINSDALE AND BACK

22.6 MILES

YOUR BICYCLE HELMET

You know that helmet use is important. But is your helmet really protecting you? Only if you're wearing it correctly — that is, *level on the head* (not tilted up, back, or sideways), with the side and chin straps properly adjusted and fastened securely. Follow these simple instructions to make sure that you are wearing the right size helmet and that you are wearing it correctly:

1. Start out with the smallest size helmet that fits your head. With the foam padding removed, try on different sizes and brands of helmets until you find one that fits the shape and size of your head. It should cover the majority of your forehead, with only an inch or so of skin exposed above your eyebrows. Even without the straps fastened or the pads in place, there should be little movement when you move your head from side to side.

2. Now put in the foam pads that come with the helmet, allowing you to get a "custom fit." Try out thin or thick ones where you need them for fit and comfort.

3. There are really five straps that need to be adjusted for a proper fit. The ear straps are first, with each section of the strap (front and back), and each side (left and right) done separately. When adjusted correctly, each ear strap should meet at a point at your ear lobe, with no loose play in the straps. **Make sure you base your adjustment decisions on the helmet being worn correctly, level on your head!** Only after these straps are adjusted should you try adjusting the chin strap. It should be snug, with room for only one or two fingers between the strap and your chin.

4. Check your adjustments by rocking your head from side to side and back and forth. Also take the palm of your hand and try to push the helmet up on your forehead. There should be little movement in any of these actions. For added confidence, try standing in front of a mirror while making and checking these adjustments.

Following these steps will ensure that your helmet is protecting your head as it was designed to do.

(Courtesy of the League of American Bicyclists).

Ride 20: *Pittsfield Highlander*
41.2 miles

This is a no-nonsense, serious ride that begins with a 4-mi. pull up the N. flank of Washington Mtn., followed by 4 mi. downhill to Becket, a somewhat off-the-beaten-track village on Rte. 8 that features an arts center, a general store and a beautiful New England church, all clustered around an intersection.

The ride then heads S. on Rte. 8 and E. on Rte. 20 for a series of undulating uphills and downhills, none of them really steep but some as long as a mile.

Just before Lee, the ride heads N. to Pittsfield, skirting both Lee and Lenox on a back road that goes through pretty countryside to Lenoxdale and, just beyond, the rail museum and station operated by the Berkshire Scenic Railway.

The ride then continues to Pittsfield, via East St. and Holmes Rd., passing Arrowhead, where Herman Melville wrote *Moby Dick*, and now the headquarters for the Berkshire County Historical Society.

The ride starts at the information booth at Park Square. To make sure the start is right, walk the bikes on the sidewalk in front of the County Courthouse to Wendell Ave., across from the Berkshire Athenaeum, Pittsfield's public library. Ride down Wendell for a block, then take a left at the light on E. Housatonic St. Take a right at the next light on Appleton Ave., go about a block or so to a triangle intersection, then left over a bridge, a short right, then the first left. Riders should now be on Williams St., the first leg of the trip.

Follow Williams St. for nearly 4 mi., crossing Holmes Rd., where there's a light, almost immediately. About halfway along Williams St., on the right, is a small shopping plaza.

At the trip's 3.5 mi. reading, Williams St. ends at Division St., an intersection with a farm stand, Burgner's, ahead and left. Go straight for 0.2 mi., then right on Washington Mtn. Rd. Almost immediately the hill begins.

Washington Mtn., which is part of the October Mtn. State Forest, is an expanse of wilderness that lies to the east of Lee,

Lenox and Pittsfield. It is roughly bisected by the Appalachian Trail, which the ride will cross near the summit. Because of the rugged terrain, the area even outside the state-owned land is sparsely populated.

In fact, one traveler in 1694, the Rev. Benjamin Wadsworth, who later became president of Harvard, called the area "a hideous howling wilderness," writing, "Ye road which we traveled this day was very woody, rocky, mountainous, swampy; extreme bad riding it was."

Thankfully, conditions have improved considerably since then. Washington Mtn. Rd. is a long climb, but the grade for the most part is gradual. There are thick woods on each side, with the road bordered by evergreens beginning about halfway up. Much of the land to the left is part of the Pittsfield watershed and drains into Sackett Reservoir, one of the features on Ride 19.

The crossing of the Appalachian Trail at the 8.1 mi. mark is a good spot for a breather because by this time the grade, while still uphill, has flattened out considerably. The summit of the road is reached in another 1 mi.

From there it's all downhill to Becket. Three mi. beyond the summit McNerney Rd. bears right, and Brooker Hill Rd. bears left with an arrow pointing to Becket. Either way will arrive at Rte. 8, and both are approximately the same distance.

Take the left, however, for Becket. In about 0.5 mi. there will be another intersection, and again take the left, for a fairly steep downhill to the center of Becket and the intersection with Rte. 8. The Becket Arts Center is on the right at the intersection, the church straight ahead and the general store off to the left.

Go right on Rte. 8 for a series of long up- and downhills on the 6-mi. leg to Rte. 20.   While Rte. 8 doesn't have wide shoulders, the road surface is good, and traffic is light. In about 1 mi. a main road comes in from the right, but keep bearing left, following Rte. 8.

Take a right at the intersection with Rte. 20, and again be prepared for a series of step-by-step uphills as the road goes over the Berkshire Plateau and heads down into Lee, a 10-mi.

stretch aptly named Jacob's Ladder. About 5 mi. along, Rte. 8 goes off to the left and heads S. to Connecticut. Stay on Rte. 20, passing the turnoff on the right to Jacob's Pillow, an internationally known summer dance festival. Then, teasing the Mass. Pike, Rte. 20 goes under the double-barrel highway twice and then over it, all within a 3-mi. stretch. Between the final 2 turnpike encounters, it passes Greenwater Pond on the left.

About 1.5 mi. beyond the turnpike overpass begin watching for a road bearing off to the right, with a sign pointing to October Mtn. State Forest. Since the ride is downhill at this point, it comes up rather suddenly. Take the turn; for the record, the ride is briefly on Maple St. There's a short climb and then the road almost immediately goes over the turnpike, then bears right on East St.

In 1.8 mi. East St. heads into a T intersection, with a road going off to the right to October Mtn. State Forest immediately before the T. Ride to the T, then go right on Mill St. for about 0.5 mi. to Lenoxdale, arriving by going over a railroad bridge just before the village intersection.

Turn right on Crystal St. after the railroad bridge for 1.2 flat mi. to the Berkshire Scenic Railway, which operates a rail museum in the restored Lenox train station. The paved road makes a sharp left at the end of Crystal; keep going straight on a dirt road for about 0.2 mi. to the railroad station.

At the left, the ride departs from Crystal St. and heads uphill on Housatonic St. for 0.8 mi., then goes right on East St. for nearly 3 mi. to Holmes Rd. A bit over 1 mi. along, look for the Eastover resort on the right, followed by a field with buffalo grazing.

An illusion of the Wild West? Not really. The late owner of Eastover collected large objects. Not surprisingly, then, he acquired some buffalo for a herd that has been a fixture of the Berkshire landscape for years..

Holmes Rd. begins the last leg of the trip. Arrowhead is on the left about 0.5 mi. along and well worth a stop. After Arrowhead the ride continues for another 1.5 mi. to Canoe

RIDE 20:
PITTSFIELD HIGHLANDER
41.2 MILES

THE BERKSHIRE MUSEUM,
PITTSFIELD

START
PARK SQUARE
INFO BOOTH

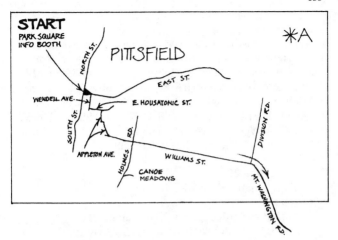

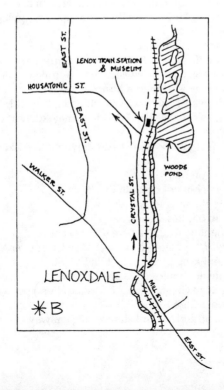

Meadows, a Massachusetts Audubon passive recreation area on the right, and then almost immediately comes the traffic light at the intersection of Holmes Rd. and Williams St., closing the loop. Go left for 0.5 mi., go right on Appleton Ave., then left over the bridge, right up a hill to a traffic light, then left again. The ride now follows E. Housatonic St. for 3 blocks to the light at Wendell Ave. Take a right for a block to the start-finish at the Park Square information booth.

Summary: Ride 20

0.0	Park Square information booth.
0.1	Go right on Wendell Ave.
0.3	Go left at traffic light on E. Housatonic St.
0.5	Go right at traffic light on Appleton Ave.
0.8	After short downhill bear left at intersection, cross bridge over Housatonic River, go right on Appleton Ave.
1.1	Go left on Williams St.
1.6	Williams St. crosses Holmes Rd. at traffic light.
3.5	Williams St. ends at Division St. Go straight.
3.7	Go right on Washington Mtn. Rd.
8.1	Appalachian Trail crosses Washington Mtn. Rd.
12.0	Go left on Brooker Hill Rd. (McNerney Rd. bears right.)
12.5	Bear left at intersection. Head downhill to Becket Center.
13.0	Go right on Rte. 8.
13.5	McNerney intersects with Rte. 8.
14.5	County Rd. intersects with Rte. 8.
19.4	Go right on Rtes. 20 and 8.
24.5	Bear right on Rte. 20 where Rte. 8 heads S.
30.1	Follow sign pointer to October Mtn. Cross over Mass. Pike. and keep bearing right on East St.
32.3	Go right at T intersection on Mill St.
32.7	Go right on Crystal St. at Lenoxdale after crossing railroad bridge.
33.9	Crystal St. ends at Berkshire Scenic Railway.

33.9   Take sharp left on Housatonic St.

34.7   Go right on East St.

35.9   Eastover resort. Keep going straight.

37.6   Go right on Holmes Rd.

38.2   Arrowhead. Headquarters of Berkshire County Historical Society.

39.7   Go left at traffic light marking intersection of Holmes Rd. with Williams St.

40.2   Go right on Appleton Ave., then left over bridge, then right again.

40.8   Go left on E. Housatonic St. at traffic light marking intersection with Appleton.

41.1   Go right on Wendell Ave. at traffic light.

41.3   Wendell Ave. intersects with East St. Go left for information booth.

41.3   Total Mileage.

Ride 21: *Two-Lake Bike and Swim*
15.5 miles; shorter version, 9.7 miles

The longer version of the ride goes around the 2 lakes in Pittsfield, Onota and Pontoosuc; the shorter version is around Onota only. Both lakes offer swimming and picnicking. The ride also goes by the entrance of Pittsfield State Forest with its camping, hiking, swimming and picnicking facilities. The ride has one short steep hill (Bull Hill) that is easily walkable, and several smaller ones, all manageable with gears.

The ride begins at the Park Square information booth. Go around the square and out West St., leaving with the Berkshire Hilton on the left. Since traffic can be heavy around the square, it may be preferable to walk bikes around the square to West St.

Coast down the beginning of West St., going straight at the first traffic light, then curving around to the right underneath a railroad bridge to a stop sign next to the Northeast Utilities building on the left, with the Salvation Army building on the right.

Go left, still on West St., for about 1 mi. to the traffic light marking Valentine Rd. at the right and Jason St. at the left. There's a small hill almost immediately after the turn. Go straight at the traffic light and up a second hill to Churchill St., 1.3 mi. beyond the Valentine Rd. light.

Go right on Churchill St. for a rolling up-and-down ride, watching neighborhoods gradually turn to country. Cascade St., the entrance to the state forest, is nearly 2 mi. along on Churchill, or 4.5 mi. on the trip odometer. (The actual entrance to the park is another 0.7 mi. along Cascade St., which climbs gradually.)

Continue for another 0.5 mi. on Churchill to the Dan Casey Memorial Dr. on the right, and ride 300 yards or so to the causeway that crosses Onota Lake. It's a good spot to stop, watch the fishing and take in the view to the S., which includes South Mtn. and the Bousquet Ski Area. There's a small pond to the left as well as some marshes, making it a good place for bird watching.

Continue on the causeway to Pecks Rd., then go left for 2.7 mi. on a road that is first flat and then curves over a hill as neighborhoods give way to country.

The ride can be shortened by going right at the intersection of Pecks Rd. and the causeway crossing Onota Lake. Follow Pecks for 0.7 mi. to its intersection with Valentine, then go right to Burbank Park, a swimming and picnic area. The shorter version cuts out Pontoosuc Lake.

Pecks Rd. becomes Balance Rock Rd. and ends at a stop sign. Go left, bear right and down a dip and then up Bull Hill, the steepest part of the trip. From the top of Bull Hill, it's a downhill to Rte. 7, skirting the northern end of Pontoosuc Lake on the right.

Take a right on Rte. 7 and come to a traffic light in another 0.4 mi., marking Berkshire Mall Rd., coming in at the left.

(The 1.7 mi. road was built in 1989 as the western entrance to the Berkshire Mall. While it was never intended to be a bicycle or a tourist road, it goes over a hill that provides one of the best views in the county, overlooking Pontoosuc Lake. The view begins approximately 0.5 mi. up the road from Rte. 7. The summit is at 0.8 mi.; then it goes downhill for nearly 1 mi. to the mall.)

From the Berkshire Mall traffic light, continue S. on Rte. 7, a section that is apt to have heavy traffic. Pontoosuc Lake will be on the right. At the south end of Pontoosuc, about 1.1 mi. from the Berkshire Mall Rd. light, go right on Hancock Rd., marked by another traffic light. The parking lot for the Pontoosuc Lake beach and picnic area is almost immediately on the right. Both are good bets for a stop if the weather is favorable.

Continue on Hancock Rd., through a neighborhood, for 0.7 mi., then make a left on Highland Ave. Climb a small hill, go straight at the first traffic light, coast down the other side to the intersection of Pecks and Valentine Rd.

Cross the intersection and climb a gradual hill for about 1 mi. to Burbank Park. Take a right and then at the fork, as the road dips down toward the lake, bear right for the picnic and swimming area. That road goes along the shore of Onota for about 0.5 mi. before reaching the swimming. There are several picnic areas along the access road.

From Burbank Park continue for 0.8 mi. to the traffic light at West St., the first leg of the trip. Turn left up and then down a hill to the Northeast Utilities building, on the right with a fountain in front. Go right just after Northeast Utilities and continue on West St. to Park Square and the ride's start.

Summary: Ride 21

- 0.0   Park Square information booth. Go around square and start on West St.
- 0.6   Go left at stop sign. Northeast Utilities building is on left, Salvation Army building on right.
- 1.5   Go straight at traffic light with Jason St. on left, Valentine Rd. on right.
- 2.8   Go right on Churchill St. for 2.3 mi.
- 4.5   Cascade St. entrance to Pittsfield State Forest.
- 5.1   Go right on Dan Casey Memorial Dr., the causeway crossing Onota Lake.
- 5.6   Go left on Pecks Rd. that eventually becomes Balance Rock Rd. for 2.7 mi.

Ride can be shortened at this point by going right on Pecks Rd. for 0.8 mi. to intersection of Valentine and Pecks, marked by traffic light. Go right on Valentine, picking up longer version of ride at 12.2 mi. Total distance for shorter version is 9.7 mi.

- 7.0   Go left at stop sign, follow road as it almost immediately bears right for dip before Bull Hill.
- 9.1   Go right on Rte. 7.
- 9.5   Berkshire Mall traffic light. Go straight. (The left goes to the Berkshire Mall.)
- 10.6   Go right on Hancock Rd.. Pontoosuc beach area is at right.
- 11.3   Go left on Highland Ave., then straight at first traffic light.

RIDE 2.1:
TWO-LAKE BIKE AND SWIM

9.7 MILES / SHORT LOOP
15.5 MILES / LONG LOOP

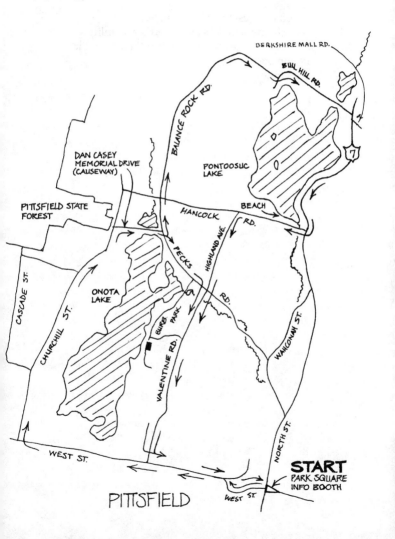

12.2   Go straight at traffic light marking intersection of
       Valentine and Pecks Rds.
13.2   Burbank Park (swimming and picnicking) access road
       on right.
14.0   Go left on West St. at traffic light.
14.9   Go right immediately after Northeast Utilities
       building and follow road to Park Square and infor-
       mation booth.
15.5   Total mileage.

NORTH COUNTY

Mt. Greylock: Head for the Sky

Sometimes described as the "high lord of the Berkshires," Mt. Greylock dominates the northern part of the county and, on a clear day, most of the rest of the county, too, since it looks down on every other mountain in the Berkshires, including Mt. Everett way to the south.

On many days that look is gray, an appearance caused by ice crystallizing on the trees near the top. The resulting "gray look" is believed to be the origin of the mountain's name.

With its summit at 3,491 ft., Mt. Greylock stands proudly by itself between 2 other mountain ranges, the Taconic on the west that separates Massachusetts from New York, and the Hoosac on the east that walls off northern Berkshire County from the rest of Massachusetts. To its north are the Green Mountains of Vermont; to its south, the smaller mountains of the Berkshires. Immediately at its base, almost underneath its eastern side, lies the town of Adams.

Climbing Mt. Greylock by bicycle is rewarding, not only because of the sense of real accomplishment it provides, but also because the trip can be made into a nice leisurely 2-day camping expedition, perfect for a weekend, that can boast views among the finest in all of New England.

Michael H. Farny, author of *New England Over the Handlebars*, had this to say about Mt. Greylock:

"For cyclists who want a wonderful mountain experience, Greylock offers the finest there is. At 3,491 ft., Greylock is the highest mountain in Massachusetts. Cadillac Mtn. on Mt. Desert may be more exposed, Smugglers Notch may be steeper, and Mt. Washington may be far higher, but the 16-mile route up and over Mt. Greylock is the loveliest in New England."

The trip is a good one because the roads to the summit for the most part are smooth and well-paved. There's also a no-frills lodging facility at the summit, or for those who prefer to rough it, a campsite on Stony Ledge Road near the summit with spaces for 35 tents.

At the summit one finds Veterans Memorial Tower and Bascom Lodge, a rustic building with rest facilities, a dining room, a living room, and sleeping quarters. Summit activities include lectures, demonstrations and guided nature walks that are all run by the Appalachian Mountain Club.

Rockwell Rd. approaches the summit from Lanesboro, and Notch Rd. does so from No. Adams, an arrangement that means the trip can be done as a loop from either No. Adams, Adams or Williamstown, or as an up and over from the south or north. However, since Rockwell Rd. is the more gradual approach, it is recommended for the ascent with the descent into No. Adams. The Rockwell Rd. approach also makes it easier for camping since it provides access to the tent site on Stony Ledge. If the trip is made from No. Adams, the climb is a bit steeper, especially in the beginning, and may require some walking.

In any event, the trip should not be undertaken unless bicyclists are in reasonably good shape. If some are and some aren't, those who aren't can drive to the top by car for a rendezvous with the bikers.

Ride 22: *Up and Over the "High Lord of the Berkshires"*
17.7 miles

The 8.3 mi. ride to the Mt. Greylock summit begins at the Visitor's Center, which is reached by car from Rte. 7 via No. Main St., Quarry Rd., then Rockwell Rd. If coming from Pittsfield, go right on No. Main St. to Rockwell Rd. The turn, which is marked with a directional sign, is 1.4 mi. N. of Lanesboro center. If coming from Williamstown, go left at No. Main St., 9.6 mi. S. of the intersection of Rtes. 7 and 43.

The climb is made on Rockwell Rd., with the steeper part

coming as the ride starts from the Visitor's Center. The pavement for the most part is smooth, save for an occasional pothole or winter heave, so the trip means settling down in a low gear, taking whatever time is needed to climb to the top.

At the 5.8-mi. mark there's a dirt road turnoff to the Stony Ledge campground, which is 0.6 mi. in. Beyond the campground the road continues to the end of the ledge, where there's a bare rock lookout. The total distance is 1.6 mi.

Dirt roads are not recommended for road bikes, especially with loads. But the trip out to the end of Stony Ledge, which is uphill a bit, is definitely worth making as it provides an unusual view of the summit. For mountain bikes or hybrids, it's routine terrain. The blueberrying is good if you're there at the right time, which usually falls at the end of July.

If you don't make the turnoff to Stony Ledge but keep going straight, Notch Rd. intersects Rockwell Rd. at the 7.4-mi. mark. Keep going up until you reach the summit. Along this last leg is a superb view of Adams, lying almost 2,500 vertical feet below.

On the trip down take the right on Notch Rd. for 6.9 mi., the steepest part being near the bottom. Brakes will be needed. Don't squeeze them continuously because the friction will overheat the rims. The resulting expansion of air pressure could cause a blowout. To avoid this, squeeze, then coast, alternatively.

At the Bernard Farm, reached almost immediately after leaving the gates of the reservation, turn left and stay left for another 1.2 downhill mi. to the Mt. Williams Reservoir. Just before the reservoir, go right on Notch Rd. for 1.3 mi. back to Rte. 2 coming out of No. Adams.

Go left toward Williamstown for 0.3 mi. to Roberts Dr., where the ride turns right, 0.2 mi. on Roberts, then left on Massachusetts Ave. for 3.1 mi. Left on Cole Ave. in Williamstown for 0.7 mi., then right on Rte. 2 for 0.7 mi. to Field Park.

Go right for No. Adams, following Rte. 2 for 1.1 mi. into the business center.

The ride can also be taken in reverse. However, riders should be aware that the first few miles climbing from the Bernard Farm near the reservation entrance is quite steep.

Summary: Ride 22

0.0 Visitor's center.
5.8 Turnoff to Stony Ledge. For summit, go straight for another 1.6 mi. to intersection with Notch Rd. from No. Adams. Go straight again at intersection to summit, 0.9 mi.
5.8 Turnoff to Stony Ledge: 0.6 mi. to campground; 1.6 mi. to lookout.
8.3 Summit.
9.2 Back to intersection with Notch Rd. Go right 5.9 mi.
15.1 Gates to reservation on No. Adams side.
15.2 Bernard Farm. There's a road jog to right. Stay left, 1.2 miles to reservoir.
16.4 Go right on Notch Rd. 1.3 mi. to Rte. 2.
17.7 Total mileage.

Loop rides to the Visitor's Center on Rockwell Rd. can be made from Williamstown and No. Adams, with E. or W. options for the No. Adams ride.

Ride 22A: *Williamstown to Visitor's Center*
16.9 miles

From Field Park in front of the Williams Inn, ride toward the campus on Rte. 2 for 0.6 mi. to the intersection of Water St., which is also Rte. 43. Go right on Water St., which becomes Green River Rd., a slightly uphill 4.8 mi. that's one of the prettier stretches in North County. Green River Rd. goes to Steele's Corners, the crossroads of Rtes. 7 and 43. At the left is a store, a good spot to stock up on snacks for the trip.

Go left on Rte. 7, heading S. toward Pittsfield, for 9.6 mi. to the sign pointing to the Greylock Reservation. Make a left, as indicated by the sign, onto No. Main St., then bear right on

Quarry Rd. for a total of 1.2 mi. to Rockwell Rd. Go left on Rockwell Rd. for 0.7 mi. to the Visitor's Center. The stretch from Williamstown is flat with a long gradual hill in the middle. The ride from Rte. 7 to the Visitor's Center is mostly uphill.

Summary: Ride 22A
 0.0   From Field Park head S. on Rte. 2 for 0.6 mi.
 0.6   Go right on Water St. for 4.8 mi. along Green
       River Rd. to Steele's Corners.
 5.4   Go left on Rte. 7 at Steele's Corners for 9.6 mi. to sign to
       Visitor's Center and No. Main St.
 15.0 Go left on No. Main St., bearing right on Quarry Rd. for
       1.2 mi. to Rockwell Rd.
 16.2 Go left on Rockwell Rd. for 0.7 mi. to Visitor's Center.
 16.9 Total mileage.

Ride 22B: *No. Adams to Visitor's Center, westerly route*
27.1 miles

The ride starts at the No. Adams City Hall and heads up W. Main St., with City Hall on the left and the Mohawk Center on the right, for 0.2 mi. until W. Main intersects with Rte. 2. Go left to merge into Rte. 2, following it for 1.1 mi. to Notch Rd., the No. Adams approach to Mt. Greylock. Keep going for another 0.3 mi. on Rte. 2, then turn right at Roberts Dr. for 0.2 mi. to where it merges with Massachusetts Ave. Follow the direction of the merge (left) for 3.1 mi. until Cole Ave. intersects in Williamstown. Go left on Cole Ave. over the railroad bridge and the Hoosac River for 0.7 mi. to Rte. 2, then right on Rte. 2 for 0.1 mi. and left on Water St., which is marked as Rte. 43. From Rte. 43, the ride is the same as 22A. Pick up 22A at the 0.6 mi. marker by turning left on Water St. instead of right as in 22A.

Summary: Ride 22B

0.0   From the No. Adams City Hall go 0.2 mi. up W. Main St. to its intersection with Rte. 2.

0.2   Go left on Rte. 2 for 1.1 mi. to Notch Rd. entrance to the reservation and keep going for another 0.3 mi. to Roberts Dr.

1.6   Go right on Roberts Dr. for 0.2 mi. to the intersection with Massachusetts Ave.

1.8   Go left on Massachusetts Ave for 3.1 mi. to Cole Ave.

4.9   Go left on Cole Ave. for 0.7 mi.

5.6   Go right on Rte. 2 for 0.1 mi. to Water St., then pick up Ride 22A at 0.6 mi. marker.

27.1 Total mileage

Ride 22C: *No. Adams to Visitor's Center, easterly route*
21.2 miles

The ride begins at the No. Adams City Hall. Follow Main St. past the hotel opposite City Hall, and then right on American Legion Dr., past *The Transcript* for 0.3 mi., until it intersects with Ashland St. Go right on Ashland St., following it for 1.2 mi., bear right at the service station and keep going for another 1.2 mi. to the East Rd. intersection, marked by a small traffic island and the McCann Regional Vocational School off to the right.

Bear left on East Rd. and continue 5.7 mi. to its intersection with Rte. 116. Almost immediately a gradual climb will begin, with some flat stages and then, near the end of the leg, a short, steep climb. The ride is marked by sweeping views of Mt. Greylock on the right, Susan B. Anthony's birthplace at the intersection of East Rd. and East St., and, near the end, a panoramic view of rolling country to the east.

Go right on Rte. 116 and then downhill for 0.3 mi., making a left on Wells Rd. for more downhill, this time 3.5 mi., until it merges with Main St., Cheshire. Go right and follow Main St. for 0.5 mi. until its intersection with Rte. 8.

RIDE 22:

UP AND OVER THE "HIGH LORD OF THE BERKSHIRES"
17.7 MILES

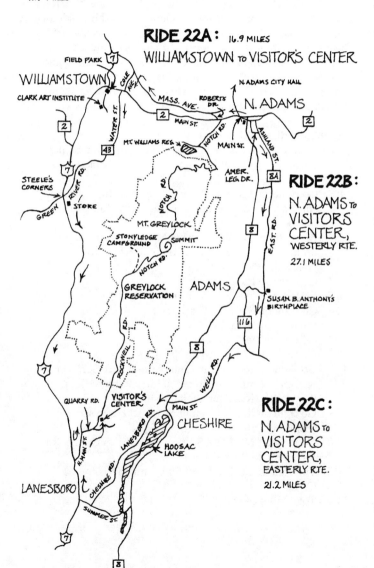

RIDE 22A: 16.9 MILES
WILLIAMSTOWN TO VISITOR'S CENTER

FIELD PARK

7

WILLIAMSTOWN

COLE AVE.

N. ADAMS CITY HALL

CLARK ART INSTITUTE

MASS. AVE.

ROBERTS DR.

N. ADAMS

2

WATER ST.

2

MAIN ST.

2

43

MT. WILLIAMS RES.

NOTCH RD.

MAIN ST.

ASHLAND ST.

8A

STEELE'S CORNERS

GREEN RIVER RD.

STORE

AMER. LEG. DR.

RIDE 22B:

N. ADAMS TO VISITORS CENTER, WESTERLY RTE.

27.1 MILES

NOTCH

MT. GREYLOCK

STONYLEDGE CAMPGROUND

SUMMIT

EAST RD.

8

NOTCH RD.

ADAMS

GREYLOCK RESERVATION

SUSAN B. ANTHONY'S BIRTHPLACE

7

ROCKWELL RD.

116

8

WELLS RD.

QUARRY RD.

VISITOR'S CENTER

MAIN ST.

RIDE 22C:

N. ADAMS TO VISITORS CENTER, EASTERLY RTE.

21.2 MILES

N. MAIN ST.

LANESBORO RD.

CHESHIRE

HOOSAC LAKE

LANESBORO

CHESHIRE RD.

7

SUMMER ST.

8

Turn left on Rte. 8 for 0.3 mi., then right on Lanesboro Rd. for 4.3 mi., a gradual but rolling climb on the high side of Hoosac Lake. The road will end at a T intersection with Summer St., where the ride goes right, climbs 0.3 mi. to the top of a hill, then descends 0.6 mi. to Rte. 7. Turn right on Rte. 7 and head N. for 1.4 mi. to the sign for the Mt. Greylock Reservation. Go right on No. Main St., bear right on Quarry Rd. for 1.2 mi. to Rockwell Rd. and turn left for 0.7 mi. to the Visitor's Center.

Summary: Ride 22C

0.0   From the No. Adams City Hall, head up Main St. past hotel, then go right and head S. on American Legion Dr.

0.3   Go right on Ashland St. for 1.2 mi., bearing right at small service station and another 1.2 mi. to East Rd. intersection.

2.7   Bear left on East Rd., passing McCann School almost immediately on right, and continue 5.7 mi. to intersection with Rte. 116.

8.4   Go right on Rte. 116 for 0.3 mi.

8.7   Go left on Wells Rd. for 3.5 mi.

12.2 Go right on Main St., Cheshire, for 0.5 mi. until intersection with Rte. 8.

12.7 Go left on Rte. 8 for 0.3 mi.

13.0 Go right on Lanesboro Rd. for 4.3 mi.

17.3 Go right at stop sign at T intersection with Summer St. for a 0.3-mi. climb to top of hill and then a long downhill to Rte. 7 for a total 0.6 mi.

17.9 Go right on Rte. 7, heading N. for 1.4 mi. to sign for Visitor's Center.

19.3 Go right on No. Main St., bearing right on Quarry Rd. for 1.2 mi. to Rockwell Rd.

20.5 Turn left on Rockwell Rd. for 0.7 mi. to Visitor's Center.

21.2 Total mileage.

Northern Berkshire: Mountains, Mills, Art and Education

Just about every ride in northern Berkshire county offers one or more views of Mt. Greylock, jutting up between the Hoosac and the Taconic ranges that define northern Berkshire. The result is terrain that's narrow valley and mountain, with the most level areas in the vicinity of Williamstown.

On some rides Mt. Greylock presents a long, sweeping majestic profile, such as when seen from East Rd. high above Adams or from Rte. 7 just S. of Williamstown. Sometimes the view is almost foreshortened, as it is when heading N. from Cheshire. And sometimes the ride is almost underneath the mountain, as on West Rd. in Adams. But because of Mt. Greylock, the riding terrain in northern Berkshire is horseshoe shaped, with the curve at the top formed by Williamstown and No. Adams and the sides created by Adams and Cheshire on the east and So. Williamstown, New Ashford and Hancock on the west.

Northern Berkshire's attractions for riders include the campus of Williams College and the loveliness of Williamstown, an urban heritage state park in No. Adams and sweeping views across the valley on both sides of Adams.

Williamstown, a village of classic New England elegance, is dominated by the First Congregational Church on its main street, magnificent houses, wide lawns and the stately buildings of Williams College that blend into and become a part of the village center.

The Williamstown Theatre Festival, with performances in July and August, has earned the reputation of ranking among the top summer theaters in the United States. Williamstown is also known for its art, primarily the 19th-century French and American works found in the Sterling and Francine Clark Art Institute and the extensive collection in the Williams College Museum of Art, which is regarded as one of the country's top small college art museums.

Both No. Adams and Adams have an industrial heritage because the Hoosac River powered the textile mills that shaped their economies. No. Adams' history is described in exhibits at the Western Gateway Heritage State Park, a restored corner of a rail freightyard adjacent to the downtown. A major focus of the exhibits is the construction of the 4.75-mi. long Hoosac Tunnel that was drilled through the mountain to the east from 1851 to 1875. Considered one of the major engineering feats of the 19th century, the Hoosac linked Albany, NY and Boston by rail, and in the process transformed No. Adams into a major industrial center.

More than 100 years later, No. Adams has seen its major industries depart, leaving the city in a distressed state, but with strong hopes for a rebirth through the Massachusetts Museum of Contemporary Art project. Although started with contemporary art as its focus in cavernous mill buildings adjacent to the downtown, by the mid-1990s the project had switched direction. MassMoCA, as it is called, is now envisioned as a high-tech arts and performance center, putting the wonders of technology at the disposal of widely different artistic disciplines.

Adams has had a somewhat similar history to No. Adams. In fact, it is the "mother town" which gave up its child in 1878 when the Hoosac Tunnel made No. Adams prosperous enough to split off as a separate community from its parent. The textile industry supported the Adams economy during the first half of the century, but as the companies moved south or went out of business, Adams went into a decline. But like No. Adams, the town anticipates a rebirth, through the development of Greylock Glen, an environmental education center at the foot of Mt. Greylock.

The town has a lovely Quaker Meeting House, situated in the dignified setting of Maple St. Cemetery in the shadow of Mt. Greylock. Susan B. Anthony, one of the nation's great crusaders for women's rights, particularly the vote, was born in Adams in 1820 in a house on East Rd., approximately opposite East St. She moved from the town during her childhood

The major attractions in North County and the rides that include them are:

Sterling and Francine Clark Art Institute, 225 South St., Williamstown (Rides 27, 28, 29)

The Clark houses one of the world's foremost collections

of 19th-century French impressionist paintings, including more than 30 by Renoir. Also included are noteworthy Old Master paintings and a significant group of American works by Homer, Sargent, Cassatt and Remington. Selections from the extensive collections of silver, prints, drawings and sculpture are exhibited regularly. A variety of supporting activities is offered year round. Open year-round, Tues.–Sun. 10–5; also Memorial Day, Labor Day & Columbus Day. Closed Mon., New Year's Day, Thanksgiving & Christmas. Admission is free, but donations are welcome.

Field Farm, Sloan Rd., Williamstown

A contemporary house of unusual design and a working farm situated on a spectacular 294-acre tract is maintained by the Trustees of Reservations and is open to the public. The land is a patchwork of cropland, pasture, marsh and forest attracting wildlife and birds. Activities include skiing, hiking and picnicking against a backdrop of Mt. Greylock and the Taconic Range. There is also a limited number of bed and breakfast accommodations.

Four Founding Documents, Chapin Library of Rare Books, Williams College

The original printings of the 4 documents that were central to the founding of the United States are on permanent display in a specially built case at the Chapin Library, Stetson Hall, Williams College.

The documents are the Declaration of Independence, printed the night of July 4, 1776; the Articles of Confederation, 1777; the U.S. Constitution, 1787; and the Bill of Rights, 1789. Apart from the National Archives, the Chapin Library is the only place where all 4 Founding Documents are on display in one place, side by side.

The library also has changing exhibitions. It is open weekdays and July 4 and is reached by entering the campus from Main St., opposite Spring St.

Natural Bridge State Park, Rte. 8, No. Adams. (Ride 26 provides description.)

No. Adams State College

No. Adams State College was founded in 1898 as a "normal school" or teachers college. During the 1960s it expanded its offerings and now has an enrollment of approximately 1,500 students in a 4-year liberal arts curriculum. The college is 0.8 mile from City Hall and is reached by following Main St. N. to Monument Square, then bearing right along Church St.

Quaker Meeting House, Maple St., Adams (Ride 24)

Built in 1782 by the Quakers who first settled in Adams, the unpainted wooden frame Quaker Meeting House stands in the dignified setting of the Maple Street Cemetery, with Mt. Greylock as its backdrop. The interior of the building is not open except for an annual worship service each fall by the Society of Friends.

Susan B. Anthony's Birthplace, East Rd., Adams (Rides 23, 24)

Susan B. Anthony, the leader of the women's suffrage movement in the United States, was born in 1820 in the home that stands on East Rd. approximately opposite East St. Because of private ownership it is not open to the public, but a plaque marks its historic nature.

Western Gateway Heritage State Park, 9 Furnace St., No. Adams

During the 1980s, the Commonwealth of Massachusetts, under its Heritage State Park program, restored 6 deteriorated freight buildings in a corner of what once had been a sprawling railroad complex. The buildings, clustered around a cobblestone courtyard, include a state-operated Visitor's Center, with exhibits that tell the dramatic story of the Hoosac Tunnel construction, a restaurant and retail establishments offering specialty and antique merchandise. The park offers a number of specialty exhibitions and community events. Entrance is by footbridge off W. Main St. by City Hall or from Rte. 8, just over the bridge from City Hall. Open year-round, 7 days a week. From first Sun. in May through first Sun. in Nov., 10–6; other months, 10–4:30.

Williams College, Williamstown

The sixth-oldest college in New England, Williams has an enrollment of approximately 2,000 students. The handsome college buildings merge into the center part of the town so that it's difficult to tell where the campus ends and the town begins, a layout that contributes to the charm of the surroundings. The privately endowed, highly selective liberal arts college has been known for its excellence since its founding in 1793 and provides the focus for hundreds of cultural and educational activities. The campus is on both sides of Main St. in the center of the town.

Williams College Museum of Art, Main St., Williamstown

Regarded as one of the top college art museums in the country, it houses some 10,000 works ranging from the 9th century B.C. Assyrian stone reliefs to the last self-portrait by Andy Warhol. The collection emphasizes contemporary and modern art, American art from the 18th century to the present, and non-Western art. The museum is just off Main St. between Spring and Water Sts. Open year-round. Tues.–Sat., 10–5; Sun. 1–5. Admission free.

Williamstown Theatre Festival, Williamstown

The WTF offers a whole host of activities during July and August, ranging from main stage performances to the late-night singing of the Cabaret group in area restaurants to productions by a second stage group to Sunday afternoon readings. The quality of its productions since it began in 1954 has earned the festival a national reputation for excellence. As a result, it's ranked among the major tourist attractions in the county. The theater is located on the Williams campus on Main St.

Windsor Lake, No. Adams

The recreation area for the city of No. Adams, Windsor Lake is located up a steep hill 1.4 mi. from City Hall. Head up Main St. towards Monument Square and the public library, bear right on Church St. to No. Adams State College, then left on Bradley St. up a steep hill and then right to the park entrance. Facilities include swimming from a grassy beach, picnicking and camping. The area is administered by the No. Adams Parks Department in City Hall, with attendants at both the beach and camping area.

Ride 23: *Greylock Go-Around*
39.4 miles; 43.1 and 43.2 miles as optional extensions

This 40-mi. ride incorporates all of the other rides in northern Berkshire, going completely around Mt. Greylock by heading S. from No. Adams to Adams and Cheshire, then W. over Mt. Greylock's southern flank to Lanesborough, then N. to Williamstown and finally E. to No. Adams. The ride may also be taken from Williamstown by starting from the information booth at Field Park, where Rtes. 2 and 7 meet, and heading toward No. Adams on Rte. 2.

The ride starts at City Hall in No. Adams. Follow Main St. with the hotel on the right and almost immediately go right on American Legion Dr. for 0.3 mi. to Ashland St. and a T intersection. Go right for 1.2 mi. past the No. Adams State College apartment dormitories to a former service station where a road comes in from the left. Bear right for another 1.2 mi. to the East Rd. intersection with McCann Regional Vocational School just ahead and on the right.

Go left on East Rd., leaving McCann School on the right, and prepare to climb gradually, with some flat and some steep places, for 5.7 mi. to the intersection with Rte. 116. At 6.3 mi. from the ride's start, across the road from the East St. intersection with East Rd., stands the house where Susan B. Anthony was born.

The toughest climb, near the end of this stretch at 7.1 mi. from the start, involves nearly 0.5 mi. that might have to be walked. The reward is a rest stop near a farmhouse at top where riders can take in a sweeping view to the E. and S. while anticipating a 4-mi. downhill to Cheshire.

Coast down from the top to Rte. 116, take a right for 0.3 mi., then a left on Wells Rd. in Cheshire, a long, easy downhill to the town's Main St., where the ride goes right and crosses the tracks for another 0.5 mi. to an intersection with Rte. 8.

Go left on Rte. 8 for 0.3 mi., then right on Lanesboro Rd. for 4.3 mi., a gradual rolling climb on the high side of Hoosac Lake. The road ends at a T where the ride goes right on Summer St. 0.3 mi. to the top of the hill and then 0.5-mi. coast down to the intersection of Rte. 7. Go right for Williamstown on Rte. 7 (left is for Pittsfield), a wide, well-paved road. At 1.4 mi. on this leg No. Main St. heads off to the right, leading to the entrance of the Mt. Greylock Reservation.

The ride can be extended for 3.7 mi. by going left on Brodie Mtn. Rd., 2.8 mi. N. of Lanesboro center, a turn that is well marked by signs to Jiminy Peak ski area, a 4-season resort. A steep climb begins immediately for about 1 mi. to the summit of the road, which yields to a downhill past Jiminy Peak on the left to Rte. 43, a total of 3.4 mi. Go right on Rte. 43 for 8.6 up-then-down mi. to rejoin the ride at Steele's Corners, the intersection of Rtes. 7 and 43.

The shorter route continues straight on Rte. 7 to Steele's Corners, the intersection of Rtes. 7 and 43, then goes right on Green River Rd. into Williamstown. The ride from Steele's Corners along Green River Rd. avoids an uphill and is very pretty because the road follows the river to Williamstown, going gradually downhill for 4.8 mi. to Rte. 2.

An option is to go straight up the Rte. 7 hill to

Williamstown, a way that provides a spectacular view of Mt. Greylock's "Hopper" section (a scoop formed by Mt. Greylock and smaller mountains) but only after a good climb. The view can be enjoyed with a picnic from the road frontage of the Mt. Greylock Regional High School grounds on the left at the top of the hill.

Whether the ride enters Williamstown from Rte. 7 that joins Rte. 2 or from the Green River Rd. (which is also Rte. 43 and becomes Water St. in Williamstown), head toward No. Adams on Rte. 2 to Cole Ave. Cole is 0.7 mi. from the tourist information booth at the intersection of Rtes. 2 and 7, or 0.1 mi. from the Water St.–Rte. 2 intersection.

Go left on Cole Ave. for 0.7 mi. and right on No. Hoosac Rd. for 3.1 mi., going straight where Roberts Dr. veers off to the right and over a hill that then dips down into River St. in No. Adams. At Marshall St. in No. Adams (the first traffic light), go right for 0.2 mi. back to City Hall.

The total distance for the ride is 39.4 mi., but if the Brodie Mtn. Rd.– Rte. 43 extension is taken, it totals 43.1 mi.

Summary: Ride 23

0.0 From City Hall in No. Adams, go up Main St. past the hotel, then right on American Legion Dr.

0.3 Go right on Ashland St. for 1.2 mi., bearing right at the former service station, then ride for another 1.2 mi. to East Rd. intersection.

2.7 Go left on East Rd. (leaving McCann School on the right) and continue 5.7 mi. to the intersection with Rte. 116.

8.4 Go right at Rte. 116 for 0.3 mi.

8.7 Go left at Wells Rd. for 3.5 mi.

12.2 Go right on Main St., Cheshire, for 0.5 mi. until intersection with Rte. 8.

12.7 Go left on Rte. 8 for 0.3 mi.

13.0 Go right on Lanesboro Rd. for 4.3 mi.

17.3 Go right on Summer St. at T intersection for a 0.3 mi.

RIDE 23:
GREYLOCK GO-AROUND
39.4 MILES / 43.1 AND 43.2 MILES AS OPTIONAL EXTENSIONS

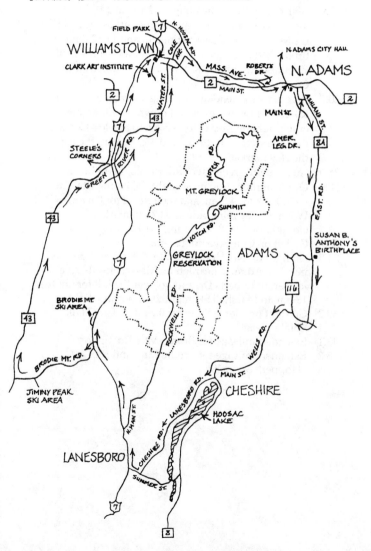

climb to top of the hill and then downhill to Rte. 7, a total of 0.6 mi.

17.9   Go right on Rte. 7, heading back toward Williamstown. At 1.4 mi. No. Main St. goes off to the right for the Mt. Greylock Reservation. In another 2.8 mi. Brodie Mtn. Rd. goes off to the left for Jiminy Peak. Continue straight on Rte. 7 for 6.8 mi. to Steele's Corners, a total of 11 mi.

20.7   Ride can be extended by taking a left on Brodie Mtn. Rd. for 3.4 mi. up, over and down the mountain, then going right on Rte. 43 for 8.5 mi. to Steele's Corners, the intersection of Rtes. 7 and 43. Pick up the trip at the 28.9 marker.

28.9   Go right on Green River Rd. for 4.8 mi. to Rte. 2.

28.9   Optional route is to go straight, following Rte. 7 to Field Park for 4.3 mi. and then Rte. 2 for 0.6 mi. to Water St., rejoining ride at 33.7 mi. marker.

33.7   Go right on Rte. 2 for 0.1 mi. to Cole Ave.

33.8   Go left on Cole Ave. for 0.7 mi.

34.5   Go right on No. Hoosac Rd. for 3.1 mi. and proceed into No. Adams. Bear left on Massachusetts Ave. instead of Roberts Dr. and go over the hill for another 1.6 mi. to Marshall St., marked by a traffic light.

39.2   Go right on Marshall St. for 0.2 mi. to City Hall.

39.4   Total mileage.

43.1   Extended mileage for Brodie Mtn. Rd. option.

43.2   Extended mileage for Brodie Mtn. and Rte. 7 "Hopper" options.

Ride 24: *No. Adams – Cheshire – Adams Ramble*
25 miles

The ride follows the first section of Ride 23, heading S. from No. Adams' Main St. to East Rd. in Adams, then a short hop on Rte. 116 to Wells Rd. and then the long downhill into Cheshire's Main St. and its intersection with Rte. 8. But at Rte. 8, instead of turning left as in Ride 23, go right, following the main road for 1.8 mi. and watching for Fred Mason Rd., which bears off obliquely to the left. There's a steady but gradual climb as Fred Mason Rd. heads N. to the Adams-Cheshire line where it becomes West Rd., a 3.5-mi. route that follows the lower contours of Mt. Greylock. West Rd. also provides a view over the top of Adams to East Rd., the route taken in the beginning of the ride.

From West Rd., go right on Maple St. At the left is the Quaker Meeting House in the middle of the cemetery. The ride heads downhill for 0.4 mi. to McKinley Square, dominated by the statue of President McKinley that was erected in honor of his visit to Adams during his term in office.

Go left for 0.1 mi., then right on Hoosac St. for 0.3 mi., then left on No. Summer St. for 1.1 mi., and right on Lime St. up a hill for 0.2 mi., then left on East Rd.

This brings the ride back to its starting leg. From the top of the short rise just after leaving Lime St. it's an easy 2.1 mi. downhill to So. Church St. in No. Adams, where the ride goes right on So. Church St. for 1.2 mi., then bears left onto Ashland St. for 1.2 mi. to American Legion Dr. Go left for 0.3 mi. back to City Hall for a total of 25 mi.

Summary: Ride 24
0.0   From City Hall in No. Adams, go past hotel on Main St., then right on American Legion Dr.

0.3   Go right on Ashland St. for 1.2 mi., bearing right at the former service station for another 1.2 mi. to East Rd. intersection. McCann School can be seen at right.

2.7	Go left on East Rd. and continue 5.7 mi. to intersection with Rte. 116.
8.4	Go right on Rte. 116 for 0.3 mi.
8.7	Go left on Wells Rd. for 3.5 mi.
12.2	Go right on Main St., Cheshire, for 0.5 mi. until intersection with Rte. 8.
12.7	Go right on Rte. 8 for 1.9 mi. to Fred Mason Rd. on left.
14.6	Follow Fred Mason Rd. to town line and West Rd., 3.5 mi.
18.1	Go right on Maple St. and downhill for 0.4 mi.
18.5	Go left at McKinley Square for 0.1 mi.
18.6	Go right at Hoosac St. for 0.3 mi.
18.9	Go left on No. Summer St. for 1.1 mi.
20.0	Go right on Lime St. uphill for 0.2 mi.
20.2	Go left on East Rd. for 2.1 mi. to So. Church St.
22.3	Go right on So. Church St. for 1.2 mi. (service station on right), then bear left for another 1.2 mi. to American Legion Dr.
24.7	Go left at American Legion Dr. for 0.3 mi. back to Main St. Go left for City Hall.
25.0	Total mileage.

Ride 24A: *Adams – Cheshire Ramble*
12.1 miles

Ride 24A is a shortened version that starts at McKinley Square in Adams, heads S. on Park St. for 0.3 mi. and then straight on Orchard St., which becomes Rte. 116, for a 2-mi. climb to Wells Rd. The ride then goes right on Wells Rd. to Cheshire and Rte. 8, right again on Rte. 8 and left on Fred Mason Rd. Fred Mason leads into West Rd. and Adams as described in Ride 24. The ride is 12.1 mi.

A variation is to start at McKinley Square, go right on Hoosac, left on No. Summer and right on Lime as described in Ride 24. But then go right on East Rd. instead of left, taking it to the intersection of Rte. 116, a leg of about 3.5 mi., then right

RIDE 24:

N. ADAMS to CHESHIRE to ADAMS RAMBLE

25 MILES

RIDE 24A:

ADAMS to CHESHIRE RAMBLE

12.1 MILES

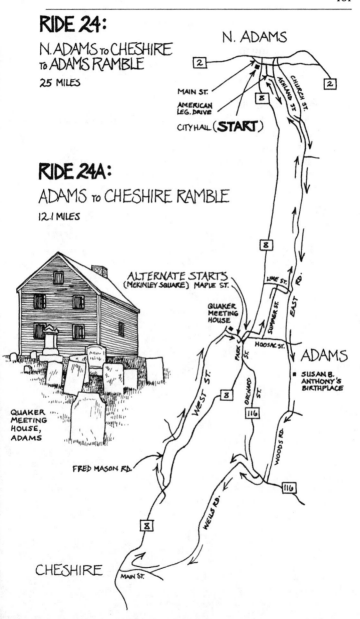

N. ADAMS

MAIN ST.

AMERICAN LEG. DRIVE

CITY HALL (**START**)

ASHLAND ST.

CHURCH ST.

ALTERNATE STARTS
(McKINLEY SQUARE) MAPLE ST.

QUAKER MEETING HOUSE

LIME ST.

SUMMER ST.

EAST RD.

HOOSAC ST.

ADAMS

SUSAN B. ANTHONY'S BIRTHPLACE

PARK ST.

WEST ST.

ORCHARD ST.

116

WOODS RD.

116

QUAKER MEETING HOUSE, ADAMS

FRED MASON RD.

WELLS RD.

CHESHIRE

MAIN ST.

on Rte. 116 for a downhill coast into Adams for 2.3 mi. Another 0.3 mi. along Park St. takes the ride back to McKinley Square for a total mileage of 7.8.

Summary: Ride 24A

0.0 Start at McKinley Square in Adams, head S. on Park St. for 0.3 mi.

0.3 Go straight on Orchard St. to Rte. 116 and start a climb of 2 mi. to Wells Rd. Go right and pick up Ride 24 at 8.7 mi. mark and end ride at 18.5.

12.1 Total mileage.

Ride 25: *No. Adams – Williamstown and Back*
21.1 miles

The ride begins at City Hall and heads N. for 0.2 mi. on Marshall St., leaving the Mohawk Center on the left. At the traffic light go left on River St. and almost immediately start climbing a short hill. Then go over generally flat terrain through No. Adams' west end for a total of 4.7 mi. to the intersection with Cole Ave. in Williamstown.

Go left on Cole Ave. for 0.7 mi., then right on Rte. 2 and up a short hill going through the Williams College campus to the intersection of Rtes. 2 and 7 at Field Park, the location of the Williams Inn.

Head S. on Rtes. 7 and 2. At 2.4 mi. from Field Park Rte. 2 leaves Rte. 7. Stay on Rte. 7, riding past the Mt. Greylock Regional High School on the right. On the left enjoy the magnificent view of Mt. Greylock and its "Hopper" section. This 4.3 mi. leg ends at Steele's Corners, the intersection of Rtes. 7 and 43, at the bottom of a downhill.

Go left on Rte. 43, which is also called Green River Rd., a scenic country road that follows the river for 4.8 mi. back to Rte. 2 in Williamstown. About halfway along, the road takes a sharp curve to the left, with Hopper Rd. coming in at the left across a bridge. On the other side and to the left of the Hopper Rd. bridge is a delightful picnic spot with access to rocks on the Green River.

Continue the ride along Green River Rd. and then retrace its beginning. Go right on Rte. 2 for 0.1 mi., left on Cole Ave. for 0.7 mi., then right on No. Hoosac Rd. for the 4.9 mi. ride back to No. Adams. If you choose to bear right on Roberts Dr. in No. Adams, which will take you to Rte. 2 going into the center of town, the final hill can be avoided. But heavy traffic going into No. Adams will almost certainly be encountered as a penalty.

Summary: Ride 25
0.0	From City Hall, head N. on Marshall St. for 0.2 mi.
0.2	Go left on River St. for 4.7 mi.

4.9	Go left on Cole Ave. for 0.7 mi.
5.6	Go right on Rte. 2 for 0.7 mi. to Field Park and Rte.7.
6.3	Go halfway around Field Park, then S. on Rtes. 2 and 7 for 4.3 mi. to Steele's Corners.
10.6	Go left on Green River Rd. for 4.8 mi. to Rte. 2.
15.4	Go right on Rte. 2 for 0.1 mi.
15.5	Go left on Cole Ave. for 0.7 mi.
16.2	Go right on No. Hoosac Rd. for 4.7 mi.
20.9	Go right on Marshall St. for 0.2 mi. back to City Hall.
21.1	Total mileage.

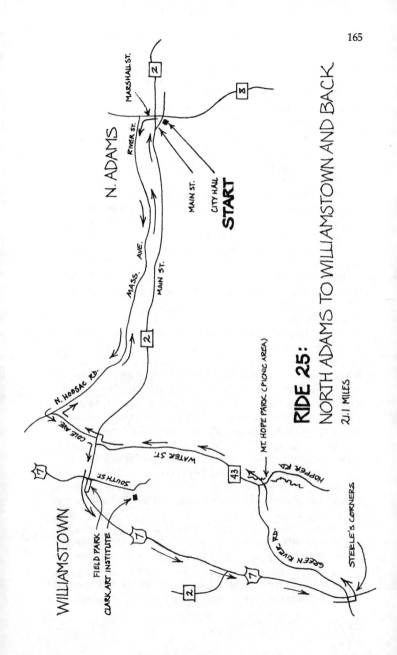

RIDE 25:
NORTH ADAMS TO WILLIAMSTOWN AND BACK

21.1 MILES

Ride 26: *Natural Bridge Excursion*
20 miles; 7.9 miles from start in No. Adams

One of North County's more unusual attractions is the Natural Bridge State Park, a 1.5-mi. ride from the No. Adams city hall. Hudson Brook, running down from the mountains to the west, has carved through a bed of marble, creating a natural bridge estimated to be about 550 million years old. The bridge is of relatively small scale and not as spectacular as its name might suggest. Yet, along with the rock formations, the site is both unusual and fascinating.

An imposing wall of an old marble quarry acts as a partial cup to the park. Many of the buildings in the No. Adams area were constructed using marble quarried from the Natural Bridge formation. The area, a state park offering walks, picnic tables and interpretive programs, is open from mid-May to the end of October.

The ride can begin either at the information booth at Field Park in Williamstown or at the No. Adams city hall.

From Field Park head S. on Rte. 2, toward No. Adams for 0.7 mi. and then go left on Cole Ave. through a residential section of Williamstown for another 0.7 mi., crossing the bridge over the Hoosac River and a railroad track. Go right on No. Hoosac Rd. for a total of 4.7 mi. as No. Hoosac becomes Massachusetts Ave. in No. Adams and finally River St. Three mi. along, Roberts Dr. in No. Adams will bear right. Go straight over a hill and then down into No. Adams on River St., passing the complex of mill buildings proposed for MassMoCA.

Go right on Marshall St. at the traffic light for 0.2 mi. to City Hall at the intersection of Main St. and Rte. 8, an alternative beginning for the ride.

The ride then heads up Main St., past 2 traffic lights and up a small hill to Monument Square, which is surrounded by 3 churches and the No. Adams Public Library, with a civil war soldier monument in its center. Go straight at the square, leaving the library on the right, up the E. Main St. hill. Bear left on Miner St. at the first intersection, where E. Main continues up an extremely steep hill. Miner St. goes left and down a hill before joining Rte. 8 at 0.7 mi. from City Hall.

Go right between 2 large mills for 0.4 mi. to an intersection marked by a blinker light where Rte. 2 goes right, departing from Rte. 8. Go straight for 0.3 mi., down a small hill, past another mill on the left. The entrance to the Natural Bridge State Park is just beyond the mill on the left.

Leaving the state park, go left on Rte. 8 heading toward Vermont through part of Clarksburg for 3 mi. to Middle Rd. Go left, past the entrance to Clarksburg State Park, for 1.8 mi., then right on Cross Rd. Follow Cross Rd. for 0.7 mi. to the top of Houghton St. in No. Adams, then ride 1 mi. downhill through a residential district. The downhill ends at River St., where the ride can go straight for another 0.2 mi. to City Hall or go right on the first leg of the trip and back to Williamstown.

Summary: Ride 26

0.0   From Field Park, Williamstown, head S. on Rte. 2 toward No. Adams for 0.7 mi.

0.7   Go left on Cole Ave. for 0.7 mi., crossing bridge and railroad track.

1.4   Go right on No. Hoosac Rd. for 3.1 mi. No. Hoosac Rd. will become Massachusetts Ave. in No. Adams.

4.4   Go straight and climb hill at intersection where Roberts Dr. comes in from left at oblique angle. Downhill goes into River St. Mill buildings will be on right, across flood control chute.

6.0   Go right on Marshall St. for 0.2 mi. to No. Adams City Hall, alternate start for ride.

6.2   Go left on Main St. through downtown for 0.3 mi. to Monument Square, surrounded by cluster of 3 churches.

6.5   Go straight on E. Main St. climbing 0.2 mi., then bear left at intersection on Miner St. and downhill another 0.2 mi. to Rte. 8.

6.9   Go right on Rte. 8 for 0.4 mi. to blinker light where Rte. 2 goes left.

7.3   Go straight on Rte. 8, past mill on left, for 0.4 mi. and
      entrance to Natural Bridge State Park.

7.7   From state park entrance, continue N. on Rte. 8
      through parts of Clarksburg for 2.7 mi. to intersection
      with Middle Rd. on left.

10.4 Go left on Middle Rd.

10.6 Entrance to Clarksburg State Park. Go straight for 1.6
      mi. to intersection with Cross Rd. on right.

12.2 Go right on Cross Rd. for 0.7 mi. to top of Houghton
      St. in No. Adams.

12.9 Begin 1.0 mi. downhill on Houghton St. to River St.

13.9 Go right on River St. for 4.7 mi., the first leg of trip.
      (Or go straight for 0.2 mi. to No. Adams City Hall.)

18.6 Go left on Cole Ave., Williamstown, for 0.7 mi.

19.3 Go right on Rte. 2 for 0.7 mi. to Field Park.

20.0 Total mileage.

If trip starts and ends at No. Adams City Hall, 6.2 mark, total
mileage is 7.9 mi. From City Hall to Natural Bridge and back
is 3.0 mi.

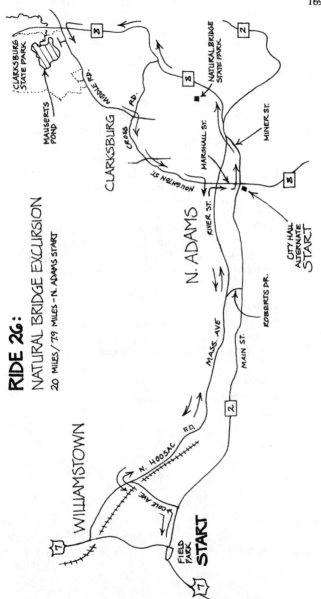

RIDE 26:
NATURAL BRIDGE EXCURSION
20 MILES / 7.9 MILES – N. ADAMS START

Ride 27: *Williamstown Short Loop*
3.4 miles

This is an easy ride within Williamstown, taking the visitor to the Clark Art Institute and through pretty residential surroundings. It starts at Field Park, where the Williams Inn and the Board of Trade information booth are located, and heads S. on South St. for 0.4 mi. to the museum.

The ride then continues for 1.3 mi. along Gale Rd., with the Taconic golf course on its left, to the intersection with Green River Rd., where it goes left for 1.1 mi. back to Rte. 2, or Main St., and then another left for 0.6 mi. back to Field Park.

A variation is to take Latham St., which goes left from Water St., into Spring St., Williamstown's main shopping street with its bookstores, boutiques and specialty foods, and then, at the end of Spring Street, go left on Rte.2 back to Field Park.

Summary: Ride 27
0.0   From Field Park head S. on South St.
0.4   Clark Art Institute.
1.7   Intersection with Green River Rd. Go left for 1.1 mi.
2.8   Go left on Rte. 2 for 0.6 mi. back to Field Park.
3.4   Total mileage.

RIDE 27:

WILLIAMSTOWN SHORT LOOP

3.4 MILES

CLARK ART INSTITUTE, WILLIAMSTOWN

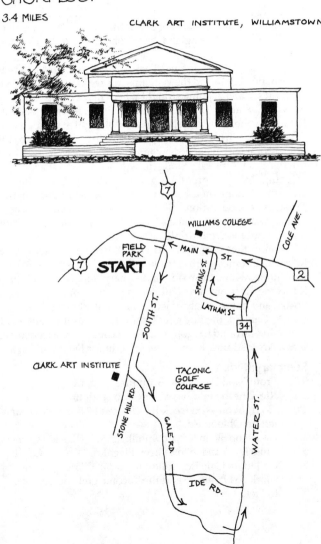

Ride 28: *Williamstown Longer Loop*
11 miles

A nice leisurely morning or afternoon tour, this ride gives the flavor of New England back roads. Part of the route, however, is on dirt road.

The ride begins at Field Park, where the Board of Trade information booth and the Williams Inn are located, and heads S. on Rtes. 7 and 2, going straight where Rte. 2 heads right into New York State at 2.4 mi. At 3 mi. go right on Woodcock Rd., flat for a while, then up a short hill and straight at the top along Oblong Rd., where the surface turns to dirt. Go 2.5 mi. to the intersection with Sloan Rd., where the ride goes left and down a delightful 1.2-mi. hill. Along the way, to the left, is Field Farm, offering hiking, picnicking and a limited number of accommodations on a beautiful 294-tract maintained by the Trustees of Reservations. Sloan Rd. ends at Steele's Corners, the intersection of Rtes. 7 and 43. There's a store at the intersection for take-out food and drink.

Follow the Green River Rd. (Rte. 43) for 3.6 mi. back to Gale Rd., which comes in from the left. Before Gale Rd., about half-way along, where the road curves sharply to the left, Hopper Rd. comes in from the right. Go right on Hopper, cross the bridge and immediately at left is a delightful picnic area.

At Gale Rd. the ride goes left for 1.7 mi. as it climbs a hill, then winds around the golf course and comes out in front of the Clark Art Institute. Keep going straight for Field Park.

Summary: Ride 28

0.0   From Field Park head S. on Rtes. 7 and 2.
2.4   Rte. 2 heads into New York. Go straight.
3.0   Go right on Woodcock Rd. Proceed 2.5 mi. and bear
         left on Oblong Rd.
4.5   Go left on Sloan Rd., downhill 1.2 mi. to Steele's Corners.
5.7   Cross Rte. 7 and follow Green River Rd. 3.6 mi. to Gale Rd.
9.3   Go left on Gale Rd., following it for 1.7 mi. past the
         Clark Art Institute and the Taconic golf course back
         to Field Park.
11.0   Total mileage.

RIDE 28:
WILLIAMSTOWN LONGER LOOP
II MILES

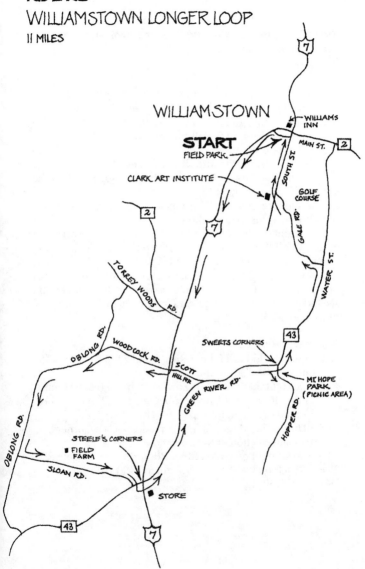

WILLIAMSTOWN

START
FIELD PARK.

CLARK ART INSTITUTE

WILLIAMS INN

MAIN ST.

2

SOUTH ST

GOLF COURSE

GALE RD.

WATER ST.

7

2

TO HREY WOODS RD.

OBLONG RD.

WOODCOCK RD.

SCOTT HILL RD.

SWEETS CORNERS

43

MT HOPE PARK. (PICNIC AREA)

GREEN RIVER RD.

HOPPER RD.

OBLONG RD.

STEELE'S CORNERS

FIELD FARM

SLOAN RD.

STORE

43

7

Ride 29: *Figure 8 High-Low: Williamstown – Hancock –*
New Ashford and Back.
28.3 miles

From Field Park, where the Board of Trade booth and the
Williams Inn are located, follow Rtes. 7 and 2 S., but keep on
Rte. 7 for 11.1 mi., going past the Brodie Mtn. ski area on the
right. Jiminy Peak signs will point to the right at the Brodie
Mtn. Rd. intersection with Rte. 7.

Go right on Brodie Mtn. Rd. up a steep 1-mi. climb and
then downhill 2.9 mi. to Jiminy Peak, a 4-season resort on the
left, with amenities including an alpine slide, a miniature golf
course and a restaurant. The intersection of Brodie Mtn. Rd.
with Rte. 43 is just beyond Jiminy.

Go right on Rte. 43 for 8.5 mi. back to Steele's Corners, a
gradual uphill for the first mi. or so but then a long rolling
downhill to the intersection with Rte. 7. Cross Rte. 7 and
follow the Green River Rd. for 3.6 mi. to Gale Rd., which comes
in from the left. (There's a picnic area along Green River Rd.;
see Ride 28.) Follow Gale Rd. for 1.7 mi. to Field Park for a total
mileage of 28.3.

Summary: Ride 29

  0.0   From Field Park follow Rtes. 2 and 7 S. 11.1 mi. Rte. 2
        leaves Rte. 7 at 2.4 mi.
11.1   Go right on Brodie Mt. Rd., following signs for Jiminy
        Peak, for a steep 1-mi. climb, then downhill to Jiminy,
        a total of 3.4 mi. to stop sign at Rte. 43.
14.5   Turn right on Rte. 43 for 8.5 mi. to Steele's Corners,
        the intersection of Rtes. 43 and 7.
23.0   Go straight on Green River Rd. for 3.6 mi. to Gale Rd.
26.6   Go left on Gale Rd. for 1.7 mi. to Field Park.
28.3   Total mileage.

RIDE 29:

FIGURE 8 HIGH-LOW FROM WILLIAMSTOWN TO HANCOCK TO NEW ASHFORD AND BACK

28.3 MILES

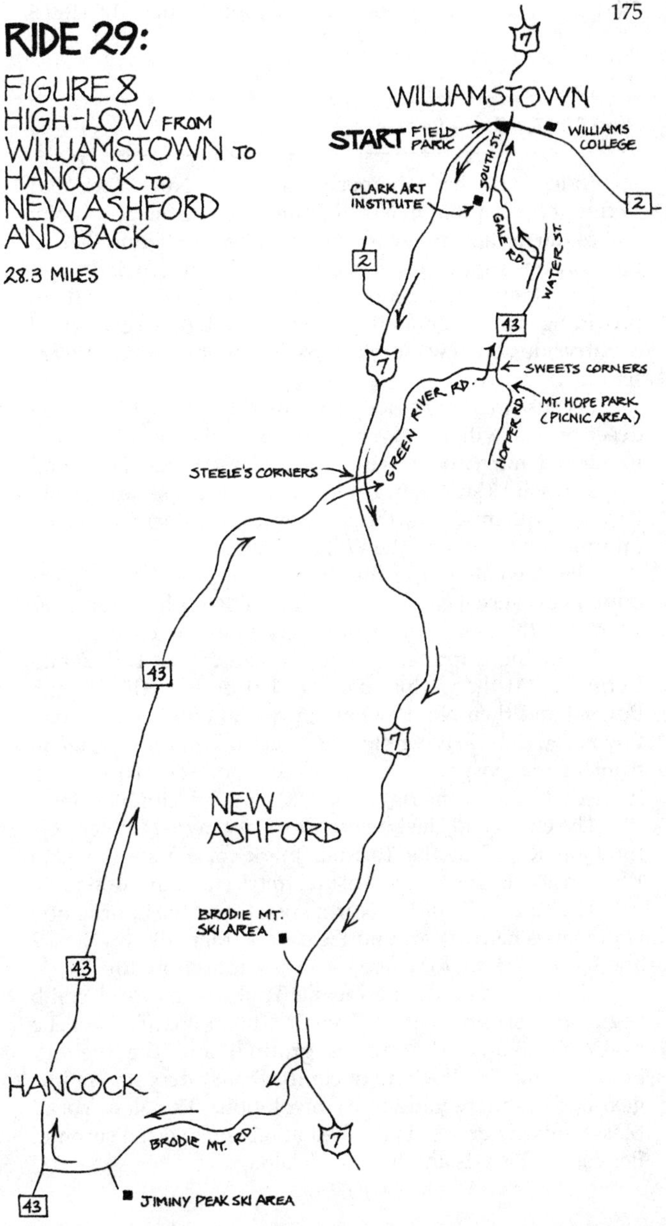
7
WILLIAMSTOWN
START
FIELD PARK
WILLIAMS COLLEGE
SOUTH ST.
CLARK ART INSTITUTE
2
GALE RD.
WATER ST.
2
43
7
SWEETS CORNERS
GREEN RIVER RD.
MT. HOPE PARK (PICNIC AREA)
HOPPER RD.
STEELE'S CORNERS
43
7
NEW ASHFORD
BRODIE MT. SKI AREA
43
HANCOCK
BRODIE MT. RD.
7
43
JIMINY PEAK SKI AREA

Ride 30: *Tri-State Loops*

Rides into the neighboring states of New York and Vermont are popular in North County, where the geography makes the terrain somewhat more limited for riding than in the more open space found in central and southern Berkshire.

Four loops can be mixed and matched, with 3 of them providing some demanding climbs through largely rural countryside with few tourist stops. Put another way, they are serious rides.

Because this book is for Berkshire rides, only abbreviated descriptions will be given, and since the routes follow numbered main roads with one exception, standard road maps provide a sufficient guide. All of the loops start at Field Park in Williamstown, the location of the Board of Trade information booth and the Williams Inn.

The Pownal Loop is the shortest but probably the most popular because it can be ridden in less than 2 hours and has 1 long hill that takes a measure of endurance to conquer.

From the information booth, head N. on Rte. 7 into Vermont. At the 4.1 mi. mark, go left on Rte. 346 through Pownal and then No. Pownal, for a total of 3.6 mi. At No. Pownal go right, leaving Rte. 346, which takes an abrupt left in front of the post office as it heads into New York State. Immediately after the right turn, a 2.4 mi. hill climb begins.

The climb ends just before Rte. 7 at Pownal Center. Go right on Rte. 7 at the 10.5-mi. mark for 7.1 mi. back to Williamstown. The first part of the stretch is a 3.2-mi. downhill.

The Taconic Trail and North Loop leaves the information booth, goes halfway around Field Park, then follows Rtes. 2 and 7 S. for 2.4 mi. to where Rte. 2 separates from Rte. 7.

Go right on Rte. 2, the Taconic Trail, and the 4-mi. climb begins almost immediately. The climb holds no surprises. The grade is steady, the curves gradual and the scenery breathtaking. It's the kind of climb where riders stay in low gear and crank, revolution by revolution. The New York/Massachusetts border is reached at 6.2 mi. and the summit, Petersburg Pass, is another 0.2 mi. along.

It's a good idea to put on extra clothing at the top, where there's usually a wind. The downhill is actually 5.5 mi. — all the way to Petersburg, NY — but the first 3 mi. are both steep and curvy, so use caution.

The leg ends in the village of Petersburg with Rte. 22 well-marked. Take a right on 22 and head N. on a gradual downhill with some flat steps for 5.3 mi. to No. Petersburg and Rte. 346 coming in from the right. There's a small grocery and a restaurant at the intersection.

Go right on Rte. 346, following it through flat country for 2.5 mi. to the Hoosac River and the New York –Vermont line. Keep going straight for another 1.1 mi. to No. Pownal, with the U.S. Post Office on the left and a traffic island immediately ahead.

At this point the ride can bear left and go up the long hill of the Pownal Loop or make a right and follow Rte. 346 for 3.6 mi., through the village of Pownal to the intersection with Rte. 7.

Go right on Rte. 7 for 4.1 mi. back to the information booth at Field Park. Total mileage this way is 28.5

To take the hill out of No. Pownal, bear left and climb for 2.4 mi., then ride another 0.4 mi. to Rte. 7. Go right on Rte. 7 for a 3.2 mi. downhill, then flat for another 3.9 mi. back to Field Park. Total mileage this way is 30.7.

The Taconic Trail and South Loop starts the same way as its northern counterpart, but instead of going N. on Rte. 22 at the 11.9 mark in Petersburg, NY, it goes S. for 15.4 mi. to Stephentown, NY. The ride never actually passes through Stephentown but does arrive at a large intersection with Rte. 43 just outside the village at a traffic light. This section is gently rolling.

Go left on Rte. 43, the 27.3 mark, and follow it back for 12.3 mi. to its intersection with Rte. 7 at Steele's Corners in Williamstown. Again, this section is rolling, with a gradual uphill for 7 mi., then a gentle downhill to Rte. 7.

Cross Rte. 7 and follow the Green River Rd. for 3.6 mi. to Gale Rd. on the left. Go left on Gale for another 1.7 mi. to the information booth at Field Park. Total mileage is 44.9.

The Loop Perimeter means a good day's ride but it also avoids the 4-mi. pull over the Taconic Trail. Again the ride starts at the Board of Trade information booth at Field Park. Go S. on Rte. 7 for 4.3 mi. to Steele's Corners and then take a right on Rte. 43, following it for 12.3 mi. to its intersection with New York Rte. 22.

Go right on Rte. 22 for 15.4 mi., the intersection with Rte. 2 at Petersburg, NY, picking up the Taconic Trail and North Loop at Petersburg. The total ride will be 46.1 mi. if the No. Pownal hill on the Pownal Loop is avoided and 48.3 mi. if it is taken. Congratulations if you made it all the way!

LINKING THE RIDES

For the purposes of organization the rides in this book have been divided into 5 distinct clusters, with selections originating in (1) Gt. Barrington, (2) Stockbridge–Lenox, (3) Pittsfield, (4) up-and-over Mt. Greylock and (5) No. Adams–Williamstown. Bicyclists, however, are endowed with both imagination and a sense of adventure. Accordingly, they will look for their own variations on these rides, or ways to link them together.

For those who like to keep things simple and don't mind traffic, there is an alternative: Rte. 7, the north-south connector for all the population centers of the county. Rte. 7 has been avoided as much as possible in the rides described because of its traffic. However, in many spots, such as between So. Williamstown and Pittsfield, or Stockbridge and Gt. Barrington or from Gt. Barrington S., the road has good shoulders, wide and smooth enough to offset to some degree the major anxieties associated with highway travel.

Those who want to take more extended trips on the quieter routes have already discovered that many of the rides share the same stretches of road, making the links obvious. However, there are 3 other connectors that aren't incorporated completely in the ride routes, yet are useful for planning more extended trips. They are:

Connector A: Division St.

Division St. is a 2.9-mi. link between Rte. 183 S. of Housatonic and Alford Rd. in Gt. Barrington. Part of it is on Ride 13, the Lenox Landscaper, from its 11.7 marker, the intersection with Van Deusenville Rd., to the 13.8 marker, the intersection with Alford Rd.

Division St. crosses Rte. 41 just N. of Gt. Barrington, an intersection on Ride 7, the Gt. Barrington–W. Stockbridge Loop.

At its intersection at Alford Rd., it connects with:

> Ride 3, the Gt. Barrington Double Loop;
> Ride 4, an extension for the Gt. Barrington–No. Egremont Loops;
> Ride 5, the Gt. Barrington Perimeter Ride;
> Ride 6, the Great Josh Billings Practice Ride;

And at its intersection with Rte. 183 it connects with Ride 9, the Stockbridge–Housatonic Loop. Ride 9 also connects easily with Ride 2, the Gt. Barrington Short Loop, and with Ride 5, the Gt. Barrington Perimeter Ride.

Connector B: Lenox – Richmond Rd.

The Lenox–Richmond Rd. goes over Lenox Mtn., connecting Swamp Rd. between Pittsfield and W. Stockbridge to Rte. 183 near the Tanglewood main gate. Whichever direction is taken, the 3.1-mi. road is a demanding climb with the summit of the road approximately halfway between its 2 ends.

From Swamp Rd., the western end, bear right at East Rd., proceed for 0.4 mi. to small pond on left, then follow the curve to the left to climb the mountain. (2 unpaved roads come in at the right, approximately opposite the pond.) At the top of the mountain, where Lenox Branch Rd. from W. Stockbridge comes in from the right, keep going straight. (A right on Lenox Branch Rd. means a 2-mi. downhill to W. Stockbridge.)

The road will end at Rte. 183. Go left and Tanglewood's main gate is 0.2 mi. on the right. Go right, and Hawthorne St. is 0.2 mi. on the left.

From Rte. 183, the eastern end, climb the mountain and go straight at the top, following the main road on the downhill back to Swamp Rd.

Ride 17, the Pittsfield–Hancock Shaker Village–W. Stockbridge Loop, is a principal north-south connector with a 9.5-mi. section on Swamp and Barker Rds. (Swamp Rd. is in W. Stockbridge and Richmond; it becomes Barker Rd. in Pittsfield.)

The Lenox–Richmond Rd. connects Ride 17 with:
>   Ride 10, the Stockbridge – Lenox Loop;
>   Ride 11, Stockbridge Bowl Ride-Around;
>   Ride 12, Five Village Workout;
>   Ride 13, Lenox Landscaper;
>   Ride 14, Lenox Meander.
>   Rides 10-14, in turn, connect with Ride 15, the Lenox
>   All-Aboard, and with Ride 16, the Estates Odyssey.
In addition, Ride 17 connects to Ride 6, the Great Josh Billings Connector Ride, and to Ride 7, the Gt. Barrington–W. Stockbridge Loop at W. Stockbridge.

Connector C: Pittsfield to Williamstown

Although Pittsfield is not at the geographic center of Berkshire County, psychologically it seems to be because it's the county's largest populated area with the most complex maze of streets. There is really no good way for bicyclists to go from North County to South County without confronting Pittsfield. The main traffic arteries motorists use are Rtes. 7 or 8 on its north, Rte. 9 on its east, Rte. 20 on its west and Rte. 7 on its south.

Avoidance of those main roads means a ride that follows a somewhat complex, but scenic, route from the south to north.

The ride, from its beginning in Pittsfield at the Park Square information booth to its end at Field Park in Williamstown, is 24.8 or 34.4 mi. The length depends on a choice between a longer, more challenging and more scenic trip, or going straight up Rte. 7 from Lanesborough to Williamstown.

Either way, the connector links all of the 5 Pittsfield rides that begin at Park Square with 3 Williamstown rides that begin at the Board of Trade information booth at Field Park. The longer version also shares some of the same road sections as 3 of the No. Adams rides and connects to a fourth.

The shorter version also passes the entry road from Rte. 7 to Ride 22, Mt. Greylock. That road, No. Main St., is 1.4 mi. N. of Lanesborough on the right and is marked by a sign to the Mt. Greylock Visitor's Center.

Ride 17, the loop between Pittsfield and W. Stockbridge, may be connected to the link without going to Park Square in the middle of Pittsfield. To do so, after coming into Pittsfield from Barker Rd. (the extension of Swamp Rd.), go left on Rte. 20, W. Housatonic St. (22.4 mi. marker with Friendly's on right). Follow Rte. 20/W. Housatonic St. for 0.4 mi., past a shopping center on the right. Then bear right on Gale Ave., climb for 0.2 mi., and go right on Jason St. for 0.6 mi. to its intersection with West St. This is the 1.5-mi. marker for Connector C. Go left on West St. and follow Connector C to Williamstown.

Connector C begins at the Park Square information booth. Go around the square and out West St., leaving the Berkshire Hilton on the left. Since traffic can be heavy around the square, it may be preferable to walk to West St.

Go straight at the first traffic light, then curve around to the right underneath a railroad bridge to a stop sign. The Salvation Army building is on the right, just before the intersection.

Go left, still on West St., for about 1.0 mi. to the traffic light marking Valentine Rd. (right) and Jason St. (left), the 1.5-mi. marker for the ride. (This is where the more direct connection comes in from Ride 17.) Go straight at the traffic light and up a second hill to Churchill St., 1.3 mi. beyond the Valentine Rd. light.

Go right on Churchill St. for a rolling up-and-down ride, watching neighborhoods gradually turn to country. Cascade St., the entrance to the state forest is nearly 2 mi. along on Churchill, or 4.5 mi. on the trip odometer. (The actual entrance to the park is another 0.7 mi. along Cascade St.)

Continue for another 0.5 mi. on Churchill to the Dan Casey Memorial Dr. on the right. Take the right for 300 yards or so to the causeway that crosses Onota Lake. It's a good spot to stop, watch the fishing and take in the view to the south, which includes South Mtn. and the Bousquet Ski Area. There's a small pond to the left as well as some marshes, fine for bird watching.

Continue on the causeway to Pecks Rd., then go left for 2.7

mi. on a road that is first flat and then curves over a hill, a rural section. Pecks Rd. becomes Balance Rock Rd. and ends at a stop sign. Go left, bear right and down a dip and then up Bull Hill, a steep but relatively short climb. From the top of Bull Hill it's a downhill to Rte. 7, skirting the northern end of Pontoosuc Lake on the right.

Go left on Rte. 7, heading N. for 1.2 mi. to Lanesborough center, where Summer St. comes in from the right. A brick church is on the corner of Summer St. and Rte. 7.

At this point, the ride can be shortened considerably by continuing on Rte. 7 for 15.2 mi., up and down a couple of long hills, to Williamstown. The connector ends at Field Park, the location of the Board of Trade information booth and the Williams Inn. Total mileage for the shorter version is 25.5.

To continue on the longer version, go right up the first of several hills to be climbed before reaching Williamstown, proceeding past the Lanesborough School at its top on the right. As the road dips, watch for the left turn on Cheshire Rd. 0.6 mi. from Rte. 7.

Go left, following Cheshire Rd. up and down, but on the high side of Hoosac Lake, for 4.3 mi. until it intersects with Rte. 8, just S. of Cheshire Center. Go left on Rte. 8 for 0.3 mi., then right on Church St., which becomes Main St. for 0.5 mi. After crossing the bridge, bear left on Wells Rd. for a steady, mostly uphill climb of 3.5 mi. to Rte. 116, S. of Adams. The road affords some beautiful views of Mt. Greylock.

Go right on Rte. 116 up a 0.2 mi. hill, then left on Henry Wood Rd. that again begins a climb, but this time you can see the top, marked by a farmhouse on the left. Henry Wood becomes East Rd. Both offer magnificent views of Mt. Greylock across the valley.

From the farmhouse at the top, it's just about all downhill for the 5-mi. ride to No. Adams. There's a 0.5-mi. steep descent just beyond the farmhouse, then the road evens out, passing Susan B. Anthony's birthplace on the right, approximately opposite East St. on the left. The house is 2.1 mi. from Rte. 116.

After leaving Adams on the left, East Rd. dips, climbs again for a bit, passes the former Adams landfill on the left, and enters No. Adams at South Church St., a small intersection with the McCann School on the left. Bear right, and follow South Church for 1.2 mi. and a former service station on the left. Bear left, now on Ashland St., and continue for another 1.2 mi. to American Legion Dr., which is marked by a traffic light, Oasis Plaza directly on the left, and the rear of a K-Mart over the left handlebar.

Go left on American Legion Dr. for 0.3 mi., past *The Transcript* on the left, to Main St., with the hotel on the left. Go left on Main St., then almost immediately right at the traffic light intersection of Main and Marshall.

At the second traffic light go left on River St., and almost immediately start climbing a short hill. Then go through a residential section that's mostly flat, through No. Adams' west end, for a total of 4.6 mi. to the intersection with Cole Ave. in Williamstown.

Go left on Cole Ave. for 0.7 mi., then right on Rte. 2 for another 0.7 mi. to Field Park. The final stretch involves a short climb, with Williams College campus buildings on both sides.

Summary: Connector C

0.0	Park Square information booth. Go around square and start on West St.
0.6	Go left at stop sign. Salvation Army building is on the right.
1.5	Go straight at traffic light with Jason St. on left, Valentine Rd. on right.
2.8	Go right on Churchill St. for 2.3 mi.
4.5	Cascade St. entrance to Pittsfield State Forest.
5.1	Go right on Dan Casey Memorial Dr., the causeway crossing Onota Lake.
5.6	Go left on Pecks Rd., which eventually becomes Balance Rock Rd. for 2.7 mi.
8.3	Go left at stop sign, follow road as it almost immediately bears right for dip before Bull Hill.
9.1	Go left on Rte. 7 for 1.2 mi. for longer version.

For shorter version follow Rte. 7 for 16.4 mi., all the way to Field Park in Williamstown. Total mileage for shorter version is 25.5. Entry road to Mt. Greylock, Ride 22, is No. Main St., 1.4 mi. N. of Lanesborough on Rte. 7 at right. A sign points to Mt. Greylock Visitor's Center.

10.3   For longer version go right on Summer St., at Lanesborough Center.

10.9   Go left on Cheshire Rd. for 4.3 mi.

15.2   Go left on Rte. 8.

15.5   Go right on Church St., which becomes Main St. Cross bridge.

16.0   Go left on Wells Rd. for 3.5 mi.

19.5   Go right on Rte. 116.

19.7   Go left on Henry Wood Rd. for 5.7 mi. It becomes East Rd.

25.4   Go right on So. Church St., No. Adams. McCann School at left.

26.6   Bear left on Ashland St. Former service station is on right. Church St. goes straight ahead.

27.8   Go left on American Legion Dr.

28.0   Go left on Main St.

28.1   Go right on Marshall St.

28.3   Go left on River St. (second traffic light). Follow road for 4.7 mi. as it becomes Massachusetts Ave., then No. Hoosac Rd. in Williamstown.

33.0   Go left on Cole Ave.

33.7   Go right on Rte. 2, Main St. for 0.7 mi. to Field Park.

34.4   Total mileage.

LINKING THE RIDES

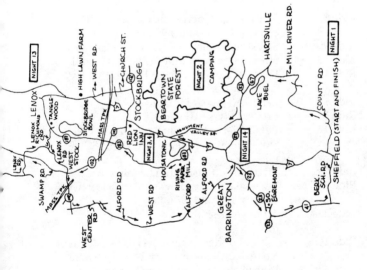

APPENDICES

RIDES BY DEGREE OF DIFFICULTY

Easy: 1-20 miles; Some Hills

Ride 2:	Gt. Barrington Short Loop, 11.1 miles.
Ride 4:	Gt. Barrington–No. Egremont Loop, 6.2 mile choice.
Ride 8:	Stockbridge–Cherry Hill Challenge; three choices: 4.3, 6.5 and 4.9 miles.
Ride 9:	Stockbridge–Housatonic Loop, 12.5 miles.
Ride 11:	Stockbridge Bowl Ride-Around, 11.3 miles.
Ride 14:	Lenox Meander (without Pleasant Valley extension), 5.9 miles.
Ride 15:	Lenox All-Aboard, 5.9 miles.
Ride 16:	Estates Odyssey (Lenox), 5 miles.
Ride 17:	Pittsfield–Hancock Shaker Village–W. Stockbridge loop; shorter version, 18.3 miles.
Ride 18:	Moby Dick (Pittsfield), 11.2 miles.
Ride 21:	Two-Lake Bike and Swim (Pittsfield); two choices: 15.5 and 9.7 miles.
Ride 24A:	Adams–Cheshire ramble variation, 7.8 miles.
Ride 26:	Natural Bridge Excursion (Williamstown or No. Adams); two choices: 20 and 7.9 miles.
Ride 27:	Williamstown Short Loop, 3.4 miles.
Ride 28:	Williamstown Longer Loop, 11 miles.
Connector A:	Division St., 2.9 miles.

More Difficult: 20-35 miles; More Hills

Ride 1:   Sheffield Swing Around; two choices: 20.3 and 16.3 miles.

Ride 3:   Gt. Barrington Double Loop, 23.7 miles.

Ride 4:   Gt. Barrington–No. Egremont Loops; two choices: 10 and 13.1 miles.

Ride 7:   Gt. Barrington–W. Stockbridge Loop, 28.5 miles.

Ride 10:   Stockbridge–Lenox Loop, 16.1 miles.

Ride 13:   Lenox Landscaper, 34.2 mile version.

Ride 17:   Pittsfield–Hancock Shaker Village – W. Stockbridge Loop; longer version, 23.5 miles.

Ride 19:   Pittsfield–Dalton–Hinsdale and Back, 24.4 miles.

Ride 24:   No. Adams–Cheshire–Adams Ramble, 25 miles.

Ride 24A: Adams–Cheshire Ramble, 12.1 miles.

Ride 25:   No. Adams–Williamstown and Back, 21.1 miles.

Ride 29:   Williamstown High-Low: Williamstown–Hancock–New Ashford and Back, 28.3 miles.

Connector C: Pittsfield–Williamstown; two choices, 24.8 and 34.4 miles.

Challenging: Over 35 miles; Hilly; or Both

Ride 5:   Gt. Barrington Perimeter Ride, 46.8 miles.

Ride 6:   Great Josh Billings Practice Ride (Gt. Barrington), 28 miles.

Ride 12:   The Five Village Workout: Stockbridge – Lenox–So. Lee–Tyringham–Monterey, 34.3 miles.

Ride 13:   Lenox Landscaper, 30.9 miles.

Ride 14:   Lenox Meander (with Pleasant Valley extension), 7.3 miles.

Ride 20:   Pittsfield Highlander, 41.2 miles.

BACK TO THE FUTURE
ON MOUNTAIN BIKES

In 1979 when I wrote the first version of this book for another publisher, the so-called "road bike" with its dropped handlebars, narrow seat, skinny tires and under-30-pound weight was in its prime.

Those bikes were fast and responsive, but also intimidating to most of the nonbicycling population.

Times in the bicycle world have changed since those days. Road bikes are gradually becoming dinosaurs, at least in Berkshire County where "mountain" bicycles and their first cousins, the "hybrids" or "cross" bikes, accounted for between 85 and 95 percent of sales in the mid-1990s. The same trend was occurring nationally.

There's good reason for mountain bike popularity. Their seats are more comfortable and easier to adjust. Their flat handlebars are more comfortable and less intimidating than dropped bars, particularly for short hauls. They are more ruggedly built, therefore less fussy. They don't mind the grit and dirt of early spring rides, and are much more stable in rain and wind. Their brakes are better, and their versatility covers smooth roads, bumpy roads, dirt roads and trails. In Berkshire County particularly, with its many trails and old dirt roads piercing the wilderness, the mountain bike offers a much wider range of experience.

About the only thing they don't do so well is go as fast as road bikes on decent roads. But speed, as it turns out, is not a big priority with most recreational riders.

Despite their name, only about one-quarter of the mountain bikes ever see the woods and rugged terrain. Bicycle shop owners report that these are the higher end, more expensive varieties. Most bicyclists prefer the less expensive hybrid, designed for dirt and paved roads and for the less rugged trails.

No matter what category of bicycle is chosen, gearing has taken quantum leaps forward in recent years. The mountain-style bicycles generally have a much lower range of gears, making the hills negotiable even for the out-of-condition bicyclist. The popularity of the three-ring chainwheel has given bicycles 18 gears and more, and while not all of them are used on every ride, the reserve is there. Additionally, shifters have become much more easy to use, routinely clicking into place instead of the guess-search-and-feel styles of 20 years ago.

Like road bikes, mountain bikes can be modified. Buy a pair of wheels with knobby tires for rough terrain, but keep a second pair on hand with smoother, lighter tires for road trips. Additionally, road-trippers who are pedaling the long trips frequently replace flat handlebars with drops. The point is, fine tuning is the bicyclist's option.

A comprehensive book about *back country riding* in Berkshire County will probably never be written. Part of the reason is that many of the trips traverse private land. While it is one thing for landowners to allow bikes on their properties through agreement with a local bike shop or individual riders, it is quite another to have the trail through their property described in print as an invitation to the world at large — including recreational gas-powered four-wheel vehicles — to use their properties.

Nevertheless, Berkshire County is blessed with an abundance of publicly owned land accessible to the off-road bicyclist. The best sources of information about these trails come from the local bike shops or from state trail maps of the parks.

In North County, there's lots of terrain in the White Oaks section of Williamstown, the Taconic Range and the Savoy State Forest. In Central County, Pittsfield State Forest, the town-owned Kennedy Park in Lenox, and October Mtn. State Park are popular. Mt. Greylock, that is reached from both North and Central counties, has five trails designated for mountain bikers.

In South County, Beartown State Park is a favorite. So are the miles and miles of dirt roads that crisscross the southern part of the county. The county commissioners' office in Pittsfield, which sells a county map for $5, is the best source of information about those smaller roads. The address is County Courthouse, 76 East St., Pittsfield, MA 01201. The building is on Park Square, the center of Pittsfield.

As for the state parks, each has a trail map available at its entry gate. Maps are also available at the Mt. Greylock Visitors Center on Rockwell Rd., and at the regional headquarters at 740 South St., Pittsfield. Bicycle stores may also have trail maps. In general, mountain bike riding is allowed on any road designated for Off Road Vehicles such as snowmobiles and all-terrain vehicles. No fees are charged bicyclists, unless their bikes come in atop a car and the car needs to park. Mt. Greylock has no Off Road Vehicle trails, but does permit bicycle riding on five trails: Stony Ledge, Bellows Pipe, Cheshire Harbor, Old Adams Rd. and Red Gate.

The Bellows Pipe Trail has good news for campers and bad news for bicyclists. The good news is that there's an Adirondack shelter about three-quarters of the way up for camping. The bad news is that it ends at the old Thunderbolt ski trail, so there's no way to bike to the top. The face on this part of the mountain is just too steep.

Many bikers like the Taconic Crest trail that follows the top of the Taconic Range north–south as its forms the border between New York State and Berkshire County. There's good access from Williamstown and from Pittsfield, even though bicyclists are not permitted on the trail itself in the Pittsfield State Forest. This means that heading south, they have to get off on the unpaved Potter Mtn. Rd. and on again on Rte. 20, or, if heading north, vice versa.

The Appalachian Trail, although a tempting possibility for trail riding, is definitely off-limits. The Maine-to-Georgia hiking trail that bisects the county and goes through many of its state parks has never allowed mountain biking.

The state Division of Forests and Parks, which manages the state forests, is preparing new maps as this book goes to press. They are expected to be much more explicit about trail riding. The maps are in response to the increasing use of the state parks by bicyclists.

Specific information about the state forests may be obtained by writing:

> Commonwealth of Massachusetts
> Executive Office of Environmental Affairs
> Department of Environmental Management
> Division of Forests and Parks

>   100 Cambridge St.
>   Boston, MA 02202
>   The county regional office is in Pittsfield. Write:
>   Commonwealth of Massachusetts
>   Department of Environmental Management
>   Division of Forests and Parks
>   704 South St.
>   Pittsfield, MA 01201

The state forests and parks within the county are Beartown, off Rte. 23 in Monterey; Clarksburg, off Rte. 8 north of No. Adams; the Mt. Greylock Reservation with its visitor's center on Rockwell Rd. in Lanesborough; Mt. Washington State Forest and Bash Bish Falls State Park in the county's southwestern corner; October Mountain State Forest in Lee; Pittsfield State Forest in Pittsfield; Sandisfield State Forest in the county's southeastern corner; Savoy State Forest in the town of Florida in North County; Tolland State Forest in East Otis and Windsor State Forest in Windsor.

EQUIPMENT AND MAINTENANCE

Fit

Make sure your bicycle fits. If it doesn't, bicycling will be a bummer. Frames come in different sizes, and both seats and handlebars can be adjusted up and down and backwards and forwards. You should be able to stand with the upper crossbar between your legs. On mountain bikes, lower the seat in rough terrain so you can take your feet off the pedals and use your legs as a steadying force. On road bikes, the seat is at the right height when your leg is slightly crooked with a foot on the pedal in the down position. Theories vary about handlebars, but in general they should be the same height as the seat and the reach should be comfortable and natural. Some shops have specially designed kits to insure correct fit.

Modern seats are designed to fit both male and female anatomies. Nevertheless, they often take some riding experience before they feel right. Some riders experience discomfort or saddle soreness at the beginning of the season, but it goes away as the body is conditioned. Often a slight adjustment of the seat is all that is needed.

Maintenance and Trip Repairs

Check your bicycle before the trip. Make sure all fittings are tight. Particularly examine the tires. If they are worn, replace. Brakes should feel firm; if they do not, tighten or otherwise adjust. Lubricate lightly where necessary.

The majority of on-road bicycle repairs are simple, provided you have the tools. Make up or buy a little kit, making sure before the ride that the wrenches and other tools fit. Contents should include a small standard screwdriver and a small Phillips-head screwdriver, a 6-inch adjustable wrench, a "Y" wrench (3 little sockets), tire irons, Allen wrenches that fit, a freewheel remover tool (again make sure it fits; not all do), a spoke wrench that fits; a small pair of pliers, a spare cable, and some wire and tape for emergencies that require creativity. Take along a spare inner tube, a patch kit and a spare valve stem. Tape a couple of spare spokes to the bike frame. And, finally, tuck a rag someplace, along with a couple of wash 'n dries or towellettes. Bike repairs mean dirty hands.

Racks, Packs and Other Stuff

For day trips, a back rack, a handlebar bag, a seat bag for tools and some bungee cords are about all that is necessary. Put a lunch in a plastic bag and lash it to the back rack along with a windbreaker or extra shirt. Use the handlebar bag for a camera, snacks, and anything else that you want immediately accessible. Most handlebar bags come with a map holder on top underneath a clear protective cover so that you can keep track of your ride. Some riders use backpacks for their extra luggage but they are not comfortable for bicycling.

Take a bicycle pump along. Make sure that it will fit your tire valves. There are two types of valves, Presta and Shrader. Shraders are similar to those used for cars and will work with commercial air pumps. Prestas won't. The distinction is important because a bike pump with a Shrader attachment won't work on a Presta valve. Don't find out with a flat on the road.

On a trip of 10 miles or more, take a water bottle and drink before you are thirsty. Water, or water laced with tea or a dollop of fruit juice is recommended. Soft drinks aren't. If it is particularly hot, take two water bottles.

Bicycle computers are not necessary but great fun, especially for road trips. First, they keep track of your mileage and that can be pretty essential if you are using a guide that is keyed to odometer readings as this one is. But they also provide such information as time elapsed and estimated time of arrival, average speed, miles per hour at any given time and chainwheel revolutions per minute.

The latter is important, particularly for road riding. The idea is to keep the rpm's up, preferably between 80 and 90, shifting gears to maintain that level rather than using brute strength. If you fall below 70 or 75, for instance, shift to a lower gear. Conversely, if you are at 95, shift to a higher gear. Too many riders waste energy by "lugging their gears," a term that means low rpm's and lots of muscle power. Use the gears instead.

Toe clips also make a huge difference in riding any distance along a road because they keep the pedal right underneath the ball of the foot, the most efficient position. They also make more efficient use of the pedaling arc by allowing the rider to exert some pull on the uplift.

Take along a bike lock. A lock and chain works best because there is always a fence or a tree around. Both should be of high quality.

CLOTHING AND ACCESSORIES

The bicycle clothing of the 1990s is terrific compared to that of 30 years ago. Appropriate pants, gloves, shirts and shoes go a long way toward contributing to a comfortable ride. Bicycle pants, for instance, have padded crotches and bottoms; shoes are specifically designed to grip the pedals and transmit power efficiently; shirts are both wind and water-resistant and breathable; padded gloves minimize the vibration that can make hands lose sensation and jackets have windbreaker fronts but are vented in the rear.

If you plan to keep biking, consider buying a lightweight rainsuit. Make sure that it is **both** waterproof **and** breathable.

The ones designed especially for bicyclists have a longer "tail" in back for extra protection.

Also terrific compared to 30 years ago is the sheer variety of bags and accessories to go on your bike. Visiting a well-equipped bicycle shop is like visiting a toy store. Even if you don't need it, you will want to buy the stuff, just to see whether it works.

BICYCLE SHOPS & BOOK STORES

In Berkshire County, riders are never too far from bicycle shops.

At the time of writing there were eleven bicycle shops in the county, with all but one offering sales and repairs.

Arcadian Shop, 333 Pittsfield—Lenox Rd. (Rte. 7, right next to Kennedy Park), Lenox, 413-637-3010; offers sales, repairs, and rides, but no rentals. Bicycles are part of a full line of outdoor merchandise.

The Bike Doctor, 145 E. Main, Ashley Falls, 413-229-2909; sells new and used bicycles and offers repairs. Mon.–Fri., 4:00–5:30 p.m., Sat., noon–5:00 p.m., Sat. Off-season by appt.

Foster, Harland B., 15 Bridge St., Gt. Barrington, 413-528-2100; an all-purpose hardware store with a bicycle section that sells and repairs, but does not offer rides or rentals.

Gaffer's Outdoors, 216 Main St., Sheffield, 413-229-0063; sells new and used bicycles, offers rentals and rides, but no repairs.

Main Street Sports & Leisure, 74 Main St., Lenox, 413-637-4407; offers rentals and rides, sells bicycle accessories, but does not sell bicycles or perform repairs. The store carries a variety of sporting goods.

Mean Wheels Bicycle Shop, 57A Housatonic St., Lenox, 413-637-0644; a bicycle specialty store, offers sales with a particular specialty in outfitting women. The stores offers repairs but no rides or rentals.

The Mountain Goat, 130 Water St., Williamstown, 413-458-

8445; an outdoor store that is a center for four-season activity; sells and rents bicycles, sponsors rides and performs repairs.

Ordinary Cycles, 251 North St., Pittsfield, 413-442-7225; also a specialty store, sells and repairs bicycles, sponsors rides but does not rent bicycles.

Plaine's Ski & Cycle Center, 55 W. Housatonic St. Pittsfield, 413-499-0294; offers sales, repairs, rentals and rides. The store also sells golf and ski equipment.

The Spoke Bicycles, 620 Main St., Williamstown, 413-458-3456; specializes in bicycles. The store offers sales and repair service, sponsors rides and rents bicycles.

The Sports Corner, 61 Main St., No. Adams, 413-664-8654; Offers sales and repairs but no rentals.

In addition, the county boasts a number of sporting goods stores which carry clothing, camping equipment, bungee cords, ponchos and other items useful to bicyclists. Nonspecialty sporting goods stores include:

Berkshire Outfitters, Rte. 8, Adams, 413-743-5900

Dick Moon Sporting Goods, 114 Fenn St., Pittsfield, 413-442-8281

Goff's Sports, Inc., Spring St., Williamstown, 413-458-3605

Kleins All-Sports, Berkshire Mall, Rte. 8, Lanesborough, 413-443-3551.

Pittsfield Sporting Goods, 180 North St., Pittsfield, 413-443-6078 or 413-442-8620

Sports Corner, The, 61 Main St., No. Adams, 413-664-8654.

The telephone book yellow pages list others that primarily specialize in clothing or fish and game equipment.

Many Berkshire area bookstores sell maps and other travel guides, which you may find useful while visiting the region. See the Bibliography for suggestions.

Berkshire Bookshop (2 locations): 164 North St., Pittsfield, 413-442-0165; 67 Main St., No. Adams, 413-664-4986

The Book Maze, Lenox House Country Shops, Rte.7, Lenox, 413-637-1701

The Bookloft, Barrington Plaza, Rte. 7, Gt. Barrington, 413-528-1521

The Bookstore, 9 Housatonic St., Lenox, 413-637-3390

Either/Or Bookstore, 122 North St., Pittsfield, 413-499-1705

Lauriat's Books, Berkshire Mall, Rte. 8, Lanesborough, 413-445-5191

Village Bookstore, 48 Spring St., 2nd Fl., Williamstown, 413-458-4232

Waldenbooks, Berkshire Mall, Rte. 8, Lanesborough, 413-499-0115

Water Street Bookshop, 26 Water St., Williamstown, 413-458-8071

BIBLIOGRAPHY

The author has gathered his information about Berkshire County from four principal sources: his own experience of living in the Berkshires for 30 years and riding its roads; the files of *The Berkshire Eagle*; *The Berkshire Book: A Complete Guide* by Jonathan Sternfield; and *A Berkshire Sourcebook* by William Carney.

The League of American Wheelmen is the largest and oldest bicycle touring organization in the United States. For more information about the league and its "TourFinder" (the March-April issue of *Bicycle USA*), write to League of American Wheelmen, 6707 Whitestone Rd., Suite 209, Baltimore, MD 21207.

Bicycling Magazine's Complete Guide to Bicycle Maintenance and Repair, Rodale Press, Emmaus, PA..

Binzen, William. *The Berkshires* (a book of photographs) (1995), Berkshire House, Stockbridge, MA.

Bridge, Raymond. *Bike Touring: The Sierra Club's Guide to Outings on Wheels* (1987), Sierra Club, San Francisco.

Burns and Stevens. *Most Excellent Majesty: A History of Mount Greylock* (1988), Berkshire Natural Resources Council,

Pittsfield, MA. Available through Berkshire House, Stockbridge, MA.

Carney, William. *A Berkshire Sourcebook* (1976), Junior League of Berkshire County, Pittsfield, MA.

Federal Writers Project. *The Berkshire Hills* (1939), reprinted by Northeastern Univ. Press (1987), Boston.

Glenn and Coles, *Glenn's New Complete Bicycling Manual* (1987), Crown Publishing, NY.

LeMond and Gordis. *Greg LeMond's Complete Book of Bicycling* (1987), G.P. Putnam's Sons, NY.

Sloane, Eugene. *Complete Book of Bicycling, 4th Edition* (1988), Simon & Schuster, NY.

Sternfield, Jonathan. *The Berkshire Book: A Complete Guide* (1994), Berkshire House, Stockbridge, MA.

ABOUT THE AUTHOR

Lew Cuyler has been a Berkshire resident since 1958, living in both North Adams and Pittsfield. During his career he has worked for both *The Berkshire Eagle* as business editor and for *The Transcript* in North Adams in a variety of editorial capacities.

He contributed the downhill skiing material to Lauren Stevens's *Skiing in the Berkshire Hills (Downhill and Cross Country* (Berkshire House). In addition to bicycling and skiing, both enjoyed for recreation, he rows a single scull, offering lessons and competing regularly in his age group.